THE ESSENCE OF

ARTIFICIAL INTELLIGENCE

THE ESSENCE OF COMPUTING SERIES

Published titles
The Essence of Program Design
The Essence of Discrete Mathematics
The Essence of Logic
The Essence of Programming Using C++
The Essence of Artificial Intelligence

Forthcoming titles
The Essence of Databases
The Essence of Human–Computer Interaction
The Essence of Z
The Essence of Compilers

THE ESSENCE OF

ARTIFICIAL INTELLIGENCE

Alison Cawsey
Heriot Watt University

PEARSON
Prentice
Hall

Harlow, England • London • New York • Boston • San Francisco • Toronto
Sydney • Tokyo • Singapore • Hong Kong • Seoul • Taipei • New Delhi
Cape Town • Madrid • Mexico City • Amsterdam • Munich • Paris • Milan

Pearson Education Limited
Edinburgh Gate
Harlow
Essex CM20 2JE
England

and Associated Companies throughout the world

Visit us on the World Wide Web at:
http://www.pearsoneduc.com

First published 1998 by
Prentice Hall Europe

Printed and bound in Great Britain by
Ashford Colour Press Ltd, Gosport, Hampshire

Library of Congress Cataloging-in-Publication Data

Cawsey, Alison.
    The essence of artificial intelligence / Alison Cawsey.
        p.   cm.
    Includes bibliographical references and index.
    ISBN 0-13-571779-5 (pbk. : alk. paper)
    1. Artificial intelligence.   2. Expert systems (Computer science)
I. Title.
Q335.C39   1997
006.3—dc21   97–11460
                                            CIP

British Library Cataloguing in Publication Data

A catalogue record for this book is available from
the British Library

ISBN 0-13-571779-5

---

10 9
07 06 05 04 03

Contents

Foreword

As the consulting editor for the Essence of Computing Series it is my role to encourage the production of well-focused, high-quality textbooks at prices which students can afford. Since most computing courses are modular in structure, we aim to produce books which will cover the essential material for a typical module.

I want to maintain a consistent style for the series so that whenever you pick up an Essence book you know what to expect. For example, each book contains important features such as end-of-chapter summaries and exercises and a glossary of terms, if appropriate. Of course, the quality of the series depends crucially on the skills of its authors and all the books are written by lecturers who have honed their material in the classroom. Each book in the series takes a pragmatic approach and emphasises practical examples and case studies.

Our aim is that each book will become essential reading material for students attending core modules in computing. However, we expect students to want to go beyond the Essence books and so all books contain guidance on further reading and related work.

An introduction to artificial intelligence is an essential part of the computing curriculum and this book covers a very wide range of AI topics in a small space. The emphasis of the book is on practical aspects of AI and examples are given throughout to illustrate the main techniques. This book will support an introductory module in AI and prepare the reader for a more in-depth study of the many interesting facets of this subject. I am not an AI specialist but I enjoyed reading this book, I learnt a lot and I commend it as a concise and readable introduction to artificial intelligence.

RAY WELLAND
Department of Computing Science
University of Glasgow
(e-mail: ray@dcs.gla.ac.uk)

Preface

Artificial intelligence (AI) textbooks seem to be getting longer and longer. This book attempts to reverse this trend, providing a concise and accessible introduction to the topic, particularly suitable for introductory courses within an undergraduate Computer Science curriculum.

The book takes a down-to-earth approach to the subject, attempting to demystify and make the subject concrete and transparent. Examples and algorithms are given throughout. I want readers to be able to start programming simple AI systems, for example, expert systems, game playing systems, programs that learn, and natural language understanding systems. This is an introductory AI book for programmers, rather than for mathematicians.

The book provides a solid introduction to the core topics of AI. However, in order to be concise, and to provide simple coherent views of topics, inevitably certain topics are omitted or not treated in detail. I hope that reading this book will inspire readers to find out more for themselves, from longer or more specialist textbooks, or from the research literature.

No particular programming language is assumed (or taught) in the book. Most of the algorithms and techniques illustrated can be sensibly implemented in a range of different languages. However, for some topics (e.g., natural language processing) the Prolog language allows easy initial experimentation. So, while not essential, a basic familiarity with Prolog would be useful. Some small Prolog programs illustrating different topics, and a number of links to further AI sites on the World Wide Web, are given on our World Wide Web page:

http://www.cee.hw.ac.uk/˜alison/essence.html

This book is based on course material used by the author on introductory AI and expert systems courses at Glasgow University, but expanded and revised while teaching at Heriot-Watt University. I would like to thank the students who made me think about how to present this material clearly, and the departments at both Glasgow and Heriot-Watt for (somehow) leaving me enough time to finish the book! Thanks too to Sandra for helping me with the formatting. And of course Richard, for keeping me happy.

CHAPTER 1

Introduction

Aims: To introduce the basics of Artificial Intelligence (AI).
Objectives: You should be able to:
Describe typical AI tasks.
Outline the techniques required to solve AI problems.
Discuss the successes and prospects for AI.

1.1   What is Artificial Intelligence?

Artificial intelligence (AI) is a broad field, and means different things to different people. It is concerned with getting computers to do tasks that require human intelligence. However, having said that, there are many tasks which we might reasonably think require intelligence – such as complex arithmetic – which computers can do very easily. Conversely, there are many tasks that people do without even thinking – such as recognizing a face – which are extremely difficult to automate. AI is concerned with these difficult tasks, which require complex and sophisticated reasoning processes and knowledge.

People might want to automate human intelligence for a number of different reasons. One reason is simply to understand human intelligence better. For example, we may be able to test and refine theories of human intelligence by writing programs which attempt to simulate aspects of human behaviour. Another reason is simply so that we have smarter programs and machines. We may not care if the programs accurately simulate human reasoning, but by studying human reasoning we may develop useful techniques for solving difficult problems.

The ultimate smart machine is perhaps the human-like robot of science fiction stories, and the ultimate goal to create a genuinely intelligent machine. We can argue about whether such a goal is possible or even desirable. However, these arguments have little impact on the practical work of writing smarter programs and coming to a better understanding of our own reasoning.

AI is a fascinating subject to study as it overlaps with so many different subject areas, and not just computer science. These include psychology, philosophy and linguistics. These different subjects contribute in different ways to our understanding of how we can act and communicate intelligently and effectively. Insights from these (and other) areas help us to get computers to do tasks requiring intelligence, which in turn sheds further light on human intelligence, feeding back into these related disciplines.

As AI is normally taught as part of a computer science course, the emphasis of this book will be on computational techniques, with less emphasis on psychological modeling or philosophical issues. I'll just briefly touch on some of the widely discussed philosophical issues.

1.2   Typical AI Problems

We can get an insight into some of the different problem areas within AI by considering just what we, as humans, need to be able to do to act intelligently in the world. Consider a simple task like going shopping. We need to plan what to buy, how to get into town, and where to go; navigate round the crowded shops without bumping into things; interpret what we see; and communicate effectively with people we meet. All these are things we do almost automatically, yet require quite complex reasoning. These are sometimes referred to as *mundane* tasks and correspond to the following AI problems areas:

- Planning: The ability to decide on a good sequence of actions to achieve our goals.
- Vision: The ability to make sense of what we see.
- Robotics: The ability to move and act in the world, possibly responding to new perceptions.
- Natural Language: The ability to communicate with others in English or another human language.

Unlike the above, some tasks require specialized skills and training. These are sometimes referred to as *expert* tasks, and include the following:

- Medical diagnosis.
- Equipment repair.
- Computer configuration.
- Financial planning.

It can be especially useful to automate these tasks, as there may be a shortage of human experts. *Expert Systems* are concerned with the automation of these sorts of tasks.

AI is concerned with automating both mundane and expert tasks. Paradoxically, it turns out that it is the mundane tasks that are generally much the hardest to automate. We can program a computer to diagnose unusual diseases or configure a complex computer, but tasks which the average two-year-old can do without thinking (getting around a toy-strewn room, recognizing faces, communicating, etc.) are beyond, or at the limits of, current AI research.

1.3 AI Techniques

There are some basic techniques that are used throughout AI – these will be the focus of this book. These techniques are concerned with how we represent, manipulate and reason with knowledge in order to solve problems.

1.3.1 Knowledge Representation

To reason with knowledge, we first need to be able to represent it in a formal manner. One conclusion from artificial intelligence research is that solving even apparently simple problems usually requires lots of knowledge. Properly understanding a single sentence requires extensive knowledge both of language and of the context. Consider what someone from another planet would make of a typical newspaper headline, knowing nothing of Earth politics and practices, and armed only with an English dictionary! Properly understanding a visual scene similarly requires knowledge of the kinds of objects that might appear in the scene. Solving problems in a particular *domain*[1] generally requires knowledge of the objects in the domain and knowledge of how to reason in that domain – both these types of knowledge must be represented.

Knowledge must be represented efficiently, and in a meaningful way. Efficiency is important, as it would be impossible (or at least impractical) to represent explicitly every fact that you might ever need. There are just so many potentially useful facts, most of which you would never even think of. You have to be able to infer new facts from your existing knowledge, as and when needed, and capture general abstractions which represent general features of sets of objects in the world.

To represent knowledge in a meaningful way it is important that we can relate facts in a formal representation scheme to facts in the real world. The formal representation will be manipulated using a computer program, with new facts concluded, so it is vital that we can work out what these formally represented conclusions mean in terms of our initial problem. The *semantics* of a representation language provides a way of mapping between expressions in a formal language and the real world.

---

[1]See glossary for meaning of many of the italicized terms such as this.

1.3.2 Search

Another crucial general technique required when writing AI programs is *search*. Often there is no direct way to find a solution to some problem. However, you do know how to generate possibilities. For example, in solving a puzzle you might know all the possible moves, but not the sequence that would lead to a solution. When working out how to get somewhere you might know all the roads/buses/trains, just not the best route to get you to your destination quickly. Developing good ways to search through these possibilities for a good solution is therefore vital. *Brute force* techniques, where you generate and try out every possible solution, may work, but are often very inefficient, as there are just too many possibilities to try. *Heuristic* techniques are often better, where you only try the options which you think (based on your current best guess) are most likely to lead to a good solution.

1.4 Prospects and Progress

Twenty years ago there was much hype about what could be achieved in AI. Some people were interested in whether a fully intelligent conscious machine could be created; others were looking forward to a time when work became unnecessary as intelligent machines could take over. Because of the initial rash promises, media hype and high expectations, people now often look somewhat cynically at progress to date. Phrases like "I don't believe in AI" are common, much as people might say "I don't believe in God".

However, it would be rather optimistic to expect all the mysteries of human intelligence to be unravelled and automated in 30 years of research! People now are happy with more limited objectives, as outlined above: getting computers to do more restricted tasks, as intelligent assistants, and also developing programs that allow us to come to a better understanding of particular aspects of human reasoning. With these more limited objectives, progress has been fair: expert systems have been used successfully, if not that extensively; "intelligent" control systems are finding their way into everyday household objects such as washing machines; *intelligent agents* provide a currently popular programming metaphor; and limited speech understanding systems are becoming widespread. So, although there is no human-like robot in sight, many ideas and concepts from AI are permeating modern computer science and current technology.

Some of the most successful techniques for certain AI tasks turn out to be based on well-understood mathematical methods, rather than theories of human reasoning. For example, expert systems based on probability theory are sometimes more effective than those based on models of how doctors do their diagnosis, while the best current speech understanding systems are based on statistical methods rather than a deep understanding of human language. It is sometimes argued that the success of these more mathematical techniques indicates a failure of AI methodologies. However, another viewpoint could be that the successful use of well-understood mathematical methods, where appropriate, is an indication of the subject's increasing maturity.

1.5 Philosophical Issues

Many people, when talking about the prospects for AI, are interested in whether it is possible to fully automate human intelligence and develop a human-like robot, as presented in science fiction books and films/TV shows. Should we expect to meet Commander Data in the future? This is more a philosophical issue than an AI one, but we will briefly look at what has been said on the subject.

Artificial intelligence research makes the assumption that human intelligence can be reduced to the (complex) manipulation of symbols, and that it does not matter what medium is used to manipulate these symbols – it does not have to be a biological brain! This assumption does not go unchallenged. Some people argue that true intelligence can never be achieved by a computer, but requires some human property which cannot be simulated. There are endless philosophical debates on this issue, often surfacing in TV shows and popular books.

The most well-known contributions to the philosophical debate are Turing's "Turing test", and Searle's "Chinese room" (Turing, 1950; Searle, 1980). Very roughly, Turing considered how you would be able to conclude that a machine was really intelligent. He argued that the only reasonable way was to do a test. The test involves a human communicating remotely with a human and with a computer in other rooms, so that they are unable to see which they are communicating with. The first human can ask the other human/computer any questions they like, including very subjective questions like "What's your favourite colour?" or "What do you think about the privatization of British Rail?" If the computer answers so well that the first human can't tell which of the two others is human, then we say that the computer is intelligent.

Searle argued that just *behaving* intelligently wasn't enough. He tried to demonstrate this by suggesting a thought experiment, referred to as the "Chinese room". Imagine that you don't speak any Chinese, but that you have a huge rule book which allows you to look up Chinese sentences and tells you how to reply to them in Chinese. You don't understand Chinese, but can behave in an apparently intelligent way. He claimed that computers, even if they appeared intelligent, wouldn't really be, as they'd be just using something like the rule book of the Chinese room.

Many people go further than Searle, and claim that computers will never be able to even appear to be really intelligent (so will never pass the Turing test). However, programs have been written that have passed a limited version of the test, where the questioner can only ask questions in a very limited subject area. In the

The Loebner Prize Contest

Inspired by the idea of the Turing test, a competition was started in 1991 for the most human-like computer program, with prizes supplied by Hugh Loebner. In this contest judges can type in questions at a computer terminal, which are replied to either by a human or by one of the computer contestants. Judges rate the responses according to how human-like they appear, and the author of the best computer program receives a prize of $2000. If the program actually does better in its ratings than one of the humans then a grand prize of $100,000 is promised. Although no-one has claimed this prize, one program fooled five judges out of ten, who all thought that it was human.

The following is a fragment of the conversation with the winning entry in 1996.

PROGRAM: No worries! Hey! I didn't come here to be subjected to bad language!
        How rude!
JUDGE02: Sorry, sorry. Didn't mean to offend. So. How old are you?
PROGRAM: That's OK. Just don't do it again. Well, should my age really matter?
        Just for the record I am 24. How old are you then?
JUDGE02: I'm 21.
PROGRAM: If you are 21, it's your business, mate! Would you like to hear
        a joke? Knock, knock.
JUDGE02: Don't much care for knock-knock jokes, but go on..
PROGRAM: No, let me tell you one first. Knock, knock.
JUDGE02: Who is there?
PROGRAM: Cindy
JUDGE02: Cindy who
PROGRAM: Cindy next judge in, please!

Although the conversation is superficially human-like, the computer program which generated the responses was in fact fairly simple, and didn't really understand the judge's utterances. It just used various tricks, such as having a store of amusing replies and using key words in the question to select a good reply. In the following fragment the program does little more than repeat back what the judge has said (complete with spelling errors), yet it sounds fairly natural.

JUDGE05: Hey did you like the funny nudes on the wallls of the room?
PROGRAM: Maybe I did like the funny nudes on the wallls of the room.
        I'll never tell. Hehehe ; ^)

These sorts of methods were first used in a program called Eliza, developed in the 1960s, which attempted to imitate a psychotherapist. These and related efforts show that is quite easy to produce a program that appears almost human-like, but that this doesn't mean that we have got very far in producing a really intelligent program.

Loebner contest, described in the box on page 6, a program that was written to discuss politics fooled 5 judges out of 10 into thinking that it was a human. Of course, why you should want to discuss politics with a computer when most humans have plenty to say on the matter is another question. Maybe we don't really want to build machines that behave just like humans, with all their weaknesses and peculiarities. Perhaps a more appropriate goal is to develop specialized intelligent assistants which can complement the skills and abilities of humans and compensate for their failings and limitations. This at least would provide practical benefit without challenging our status as uniquely intelligent beings.

1.6 Summary

- AI is concerned with attempts to produce programs to do tasks which require human intelligence.
- Reasons for doing AI include both the goal of understanding human intelligence better and the goal of developing useful, smarter computer programs.
- AI tasks involve both *mundane* tasks which people can do very easily (e.g., understanding language) and *expert* tasks which require specialist knowledge (e.g., medical diagnosis).
- AI has been successful in limited tasks, but it is unclear whether a really human-like intelligent robot is possible or desirable.

1.7 Further Reading

This book provides only a basic introduction to artificial intelligence. There are many excellent books which go into the subject in more depth. I would particularly recommend the following longer textbooks:

Rich, Elaine & Knight, Kevin, *Artificial Intelligence (second edition)*, McGraw-Hill, 1991. This book has become something of a standard, building on the success of an earlier edition by Rich. It provides a sound theoretical basis, though is limited in practical examples.

Luger, George, F. & Stubblefield, William, A. *Artificial Intelligence: Structures and Strategies for Complex Problem Solving*, Benjamin/Cummings Publishing, 1993. This book has a slightly more applied flavour, gives an introduction to and examples in the main AI programming languages, and has good introductions to expert systems and machine learning.

Ginsberg, Matt, *Essentials of Artificial Intelligence*, Morgan Kaufmann, 1993. Another somewhat theoretically oriented book, with an emphasis on logic-based approaches. A little more up to date than Rich & Knight, and enthusiastic in style.

Russell, Stuart & Norvig, Peter, *Artificial Intelligence: A Modern Approach*, Prentice Hall, 1995. A good, modern introduction with the theme of developing an intelligent agent. Extensive sections on reasoning and decision making under uncertainty, and on machine learning, as well as the standard topics.

Pratt, Ian, *Artificial Intelligence*, Macmillan, 1994. A good short book that focuses on *inference* as its central theme. It does not cover topics such as natural language, expert systems or vision, but provides a good formal coverage of some foundational topics. Some understanding of logic is assumed, but a brief appendix is included.

Two other good sources of clear articles by various experts in the field are the *Encyclopaedia of Artificial Intelligence* (Shapiro, 1992) and the *Handbook of Artificial Intelligence* (Barr & Feigenbaum, 1982), although the latter is now getting a little out of date.

1.8   Exercises

1. List the skills and knowledge required to successfully do the following everyday tasks: reading a book; crossing the road; ordering a pizza; arranging a trip to the cinema.

2. Suggest two expert tasks, other than those listed in the chapter, which you think might be suitable for an expert system. Describe why you think it would be useful to automate the tasks, and what knowledge you think the system would need.

3. Suppose you had to develop a program to suggest good road routes between two given cities. State what knowledge would be required for such a system, and suggest how it might be represented. Try to sketch an algorithm that could be used to find a good route.

4. If you were a judge in the Loebner contest what questions would you ask to determine whether you were communicating with a computer or a human? Suggest some possible answers that a program might give to tricky questions that would seem human-like, but which avoid answering the question.

CHAPTER 2

Knowledge Representation and Inference

Aims:	To introduce and compare the main knowledge representation methods used in AI: rules, frames and semantic networks, and logic.
Objectives:	You should be able to:
	Use the different knowledge representation methods to represent fragments of knowledge, given an English description of that knowledge.
	Show how new facts can be *inferred* in the different methods.
	Discuss the advantages and disadvantages of different methods.
Prerequisites:	It will help if you have had some introduction to predicate logic and to a programming language.

2.1   Introduction

One of the assumptions underlying most work in artificial intelligence is that intelligent behaviour can be achieved through the manipulation of *symbol structures* representing bits of knowledge. For example, we could use the symbol red to denote a particular colour, the symbol alisons-car to denote my car, and the symbol structure red(alisons-car) to denote the fact that my car is red. An AI program could use this fact and maybe draw conclusions about the personality of the owner[1].

In principle the symbol structures could be represented on any physical medium – we could develop a (very slow) intelligent machine made out of empty beer cans (plus something to move the beer cans around). However, computers make this

---

[1]In fact my car is a kind of greyish green. Draw your own conclusions.

9

much easier; we can represent facts using data structures, and write program code to reason with them.

Knowledge representation languages have been developed to make this easier. These are special notations that make it easy to represent and reason with complex knowledge about the world. Rather than represent everything using the basic data structures of a language like C++ or Pascal we can use these high-level formalisms. The knowledge representation languages may themselves be implemented using any programming language, so a fact like `red(alisons-car)` may end up being represented as a collection of conventional data structures, but the AI programmer doesn't have to know this, and doesn't have to re-invent basic methods for representing complex knowledge.

This chapter will introduce the main approaches to knowledge representation and some of the major issues involved. The later chapters will consider more how we can actually *use* that knowledge to intelligently solve problems.

2.1.1   Requirements for Knowledge Representation Languages

Before we talk about the different languages that are used, we should consider what we are looking for in a knowledge representation language. A knowledge representation language should allow you to represent *adequately complex facts* in a *clear and precise* yet *natural* way, and in a way that easily allows you to *deduce new facts* from your existing knowledge. These requirements are examined further below.

The ability to represent adequately complex facts is referred to as the *representational adequacy* of a language. Some facts are hard to represent. Or to be more precise, some facts are hard to represent in a way that allows those facts to be reasoned with. For example, a simple fact like "John believes no-one likes brussel sprouts" can be represented as a simple string, using the English language. But how can we reason with this representation, and conclude that John believes Mary doesn't like brussel sprouts? Some knowledge representation languages will allow complex facts like this to be represented in a structured way so they can be reasoned with. Some will only allow simpler facts to be represented. If the simpler language will do the job, it may be easier to use and more efficient to reason with.

The requirement for a clear and precise way of representing knowledge means that we need to have a *well-defined syntax and semantics*. We have to know what the allowable expressions are in the language, and what they mean. Let's suppose we've defined what each of the symbols that we use refers to (e.g., `red` refers to the property of being the colour red, `alisons-car` refers to my car). The syntax of the language defines the allowable structures of the language (e.g., `red(alisons-car)` is OK, `alisons-car(grey & green)` is not). The semantics of the language tells you what a particular structure means (e.g., `red(alisons-car)` means that my car is red, rather than being an instruction to spray my car red).

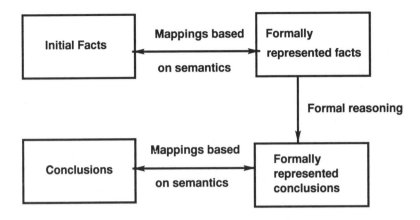

Figure 2.1 *Representations and Mappings.*

A precise semantics is particularly important given that an AI program will be reasoning with the knowledge and drawing new conclusions. To solve an AI problem we first have to work out how to represent the real world knowledge using our representation language. Then our AI program churns away, inferring new facts and coming to some conclusions. It is clearly vital that we can interpret what these conclusions mean, in terms of our real world problem. If the system concludes interest(alison, high) we'd need to know that this refers to my personality, not my mortgage. This is illustrated in Figure 2.1.

It is not enough to have a precise syntax and semantics if this means that your representation scheme is non-intuitive and difficult to use and understand. So we also require that our representation scheme is reasonably *natural*, capturing the structure of knowledge in an obvious way. Also, given a knowledge representation scheme, it is also important to choose *names* for symbols that are meaningful. We could represent the fact "if someone has a headache they should take aspirin" as, say, if(x,h,a), but something like IF symptom(X, headache) THEN medication(X, aspirin) is a good deal more readable and easier to deal with.

The final requirement, being able to deducing new facts from existing knowledge, is referred to as *inferential adequacy* . A knowledge representation language must support inference. We can't represent explicitly everything that the system might ever need to know – some things should be left implicit, to be deduced by the system as and when needed in problem solving. For example, suppose some system needs knowledge about a hundred students. All of them, let's say, attend lectures, take exams, and receive a grant. It would be wasteful to record these facts for each and every student. It is much better to just record that these facts are true for all students. When the system needs to know, say, whether a particular student Fred attends lectures it should be able to deduce this from the general statement and from the fact that Fred is a student. This obviously saves on a lot of unnecessary storage.

Some inferences may be a little more complex. Maybe we want to know whether Fred is prime minister of Great Britain. If we know that only one person can be prime minister at once, and that Tony Blair is currently prime minister, then we should be able to deduce that therefore Fred can't be. We don't need to record this fact explicitly.

Making arbitrary deductions from existing knowledge is a complex process. The more sophisticated the deductions required, the longer they are likely to take. There is a tradeoff between *inferential adequacy* (what we can infer) and *inferential efficiency* (how quickly we can infer it), so we may choose to have a language where simple inferences can be made quickly, although complex ones are not possible.

We can summarize the general requirements for a knowledge representation language as follows:

Representational Adequacy: It should allow you to represent all the knowledge that you need to reason with.

Inferential Adequacy: It should allow new knowledge to be inferred from a basic set of facts.

Inferential Efficiency: Inferences should be made efficiently.

Clear Syntax and Semantics: We should know what the allowable expressions of the language are and what they mean.

Naturalness: The language should be reasonably natural and easy to use.

However, no one representation language satisfies all these requirements perfectly. In practice the choice of language depends on the reasoning task (just as the choice of a programming language depends on the problem). Given a particular task it will generally be necessary to choose an appropriate language given the particular requirements of the application.

In the rest of this chapter the main approaches are outlined, along with their advantages and disadvantages.

2.1.2   Introducing the Main Approaches

Broadly speaking, there are three main approaches to knowledge representation in AI. The most important is arguably the use of logic to represent things. For example, we could use predicate logic to represent the sentence "All birds fly" as $\forall X \, (bird(X) \rightarrow flies(X))$.

A logic, almost by definition, has a well-defined syntax and semantics and is concerned with truth preserving inference, so seems like a good candidate as a method to represent and reason with knowledge. However, using logic to represent things has problems. First, it may not be very efficient – if we just want a very restricted class of inferences, we may not want the full power of a logic-based theorem prover, for example. Second, representing some common-sense things in a logic can be very hard. Representing and reasoning with anything that involves time, beliefs or uncertainty is hard in predicate logic. There are special logics, such as *temporal* and *modal* logics, which allow such things to be represented, but reasoning in such logics may not be efficient.

An alternative is to use simpler and more natural representation schemes, specifying the algorithms for manipulating the knowledge, but not necessarily giving a formal account of the semantics of the language. *Frames* and *semantic networks* provide a natural way of representing factual knowledge about classes of object and their properties. Knowledge is represented as a collection of objects and relations, the most important relations being the *subclass* and *instance* relations. The subclass relation says (as you might expect) that one class is a subclass of another, while the instance relation says that some individual belongs to some class. So Fred Bloggs is an *instance* of the class representing AI students, while the class of AI students is a *subclass* of the class of students in general[2]. We can then define property *inheritance*, so that, by *default*, Fred inherits all the typical attributes of AI students, and AI students inherit typical attributes of students in general. We'll go into this in much more detail below.

Another important method for representing knowledge is the use of IF–THEN or *condition-action* rules, within a *rule-based system*[3]. A condition-action rule specifies what to do under what circumstances. For example, we could have a rule IF fire THEN shout-help. A rule-based language will provide algorithms for reasoning with such rules, so that new conclusions can be drawn in a controlled manner. Although condition-action rules may be similar to logical implications (e.g., $fire \rightarrow shout\_help$), the emphasis of rule-based representation languages tends to be different, with more emphasis on what you do with the rules and less on what they mean – we say that *procedural* aspects are emphasized rather than *declarative* ones. Condition-action rules are widely used in expert systems, providing a fairly flexible way of representing expert knowledge and efficient techniques for reasoning with this knowledge.

The rest of this chapter describes these different knowledge representation languages in more detail. We'll start with frames and semantic networks, as these are fairly easy to understand. Then we'll talk about logic, and then rule-based systems. The discussion of rules should lead naturally into the next chapter on expert systems.

---

[2]The terms *subclass* and *instance* are not the only terms used for these relations, so don't be put off if other terms (such as *isa* and *member*) are used in another text.

[3]The terms *production rule* and *production system* are often used, largely for historical reasons.

2.2   Semantic Networks and Frames

Semantic networks and frames provide a simple and intuitive way of representing facts about objects. Both schemes allow you to represent *classes* (or categories) of objects and relations between objects, and draw simple inferences based on this knowledge. There is little difference in practice between semantic networks and frames, just different notations used to represent the knowledge. We'll therefore briefly introduce the two approaches, and then talk about general issues common to them both.

2.2.1   Semantic Networks

Semantic networks were originally developed in the early 1960s to represent the meaning of English words. They have since been used more widely for representing knowledge.

In a semantic network knowledge is represented as a graph[4], where the nodes in the graph represent concepts, and the links represent relations between concepts. The most important relations between concepts are *subclass* relations between classes, and *instance* relations between particular object instances and their parent class. However, any other relations are allowed, such as *has-part, colour* etc, allowing properties of objects (and categories of objects) to be represented. So, to represent some knowledge about animals (as AI people so often do) we might have the network in Figure 2.2.

This network represents the fact that mammals and reptiles are animals, that mammals have heads, an elephant is a large grey mammal, Clyde and Nellie are both elephants, and that Nellie likes apples. The subclass relations define a *class hierarchy* (in this case very simple).

The subclass and instance relations may be used to derive new information which is not explicitly represented. We should be able to conclude that Clyde and Nellie both have a head, and are large and grey. They *inherit* properties from their parent classes. Semantic networks normally allow efficient inheritance-based inferences using special purpose algorithms.

When semantic networks became popular in the 1970s there was much discussion about what the nodes and relations really meant. People were using them in subtly different ways, which led to much confusion. For example, a node such as *elephant* might be used to represent the class of all elephants or just a typical elephant. Saying that an elephant *has_part* head could mean that every elephant has some particular head, that every elephant has some kind of head, that some elephant has some kind of head, that a typical elephant has some kind of head, and so on. In this case it is the second of these which seems sensible, but for representing other things other meanings may seem appropriate.

However, if a relation can mean one thing when representing facts about ele-

---

[4]If you are not familiar with graphs in computer science, see Section 4.2.1.

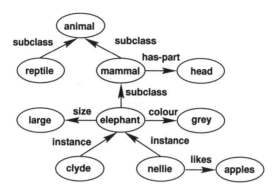

Figure 2.2 *A Simple Semantic Network.*

phants, and another thing when representing facts about, say, diseases, then chaos will ensue. No one will be quite sure what the representation means, and it will be unclear what *inferences* can be drawn from the knowledge if we don't even know what expressions in the language mean.

It is now recognized that it is important to state, as precisely as possible, the *semantics* of a representation language, so we know exactly what expressions mean and which inferences are sound. One simple way to describe precisely the meaning of nodes and links in a semantic network is in terms of set theory. We interpret a class node as denoting a set of objects. So, an *elephant* node denotes the set of all elephants. Nodes such as *Clyde* and *Nellie* denote individuals. So the *instance* relationship can be defined in terms of set membership (Nellie is a member of the set of all elephants), while the *subclass* relation can be defined in terms of a subset relation – the set of all elephants is a subset of the set of all mammals. Saying that elephants are grey means (in this simple model) that every individual in the set of elephants is grey (so Clyde can't be pink).

Semantic networks are still used in AI today. Example systems are SNePS and conceptual graphs, which both provide a precise semantics for the nodes and links in the network. Conceptual graphs are described in (Luger & Stubblefield, 1993) (ch.9.3).

Semantic networks allow us to represent knowledge about objects and relations between objects in a simple and fairly intuitive way. The conventional graphical notation allows us to quickly see how the knowledge is organized. The sort of inferences that are normally supported is very restricted – just inheritance of properties – but this means that it is very easy to work out what is going on. So, while the notation may be ill suited where very complex knowledge representation and reasoning is required, it may be a good choice for certain problems.

2.2.2 Frames

Frames are a variant of semantic networks, and a popular way to represent facts in an expert system. All the information relevant to a particular concept is stored in a single complex entity (called a frame). Superficially, frames look pretty much like record (or struct) data structures. However frames, at the very least, support inheritance.

Three simple frames representing some of our knowledge about elephants are given in Figure 2.3. Mammal, Elephant and Nellie are *objects* in the frame system. Properties, such as colour and size, are sometimes referred to as *slots*, and grey, large etc. as *slot values*. We can infer, using inheritance, that Nellie is large, grey and has a head, as well as liking apples.

Some of the terminology and ideas used for frame systems has since been adopted for object oriented programming, which also deals with classes and inheritance. Object oriented programming languages were influenced by frame systems, but they tend to be used for slightly different things – to write programs to manipulate specific "objects" in well-defined ways, rather than to represent knowledge about conceptual categories.

It is straightforward to translate between semantic network and frame based representations. Nodes in the semantic network become objects in the frame system, links become slots, and the node the other end of the link becomes the slot value. The rest of this section will use examples based on frames, but the same points could equally be made about semantic networks. The choice between the two is largely a matter of preference between the way the information is visualized.

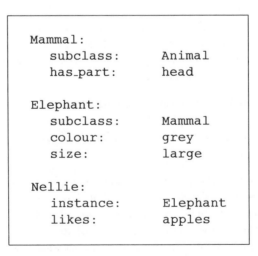

```
Mammal:
    subclass:       Animal
    has_part:       head

Elephant:
    subclass:       Mammal
    colour:         grey
    size:           large

Nellie:
    instance:       Elephant
    likes:          apples
```

Figure 2.3 *Elephant Frames.*

2.2.3 Defaults and Multiple Inheritance

In the examples so far objects (such as Nellie) inherit *all* the properties of their parent class. So Nellie must be grey and large. However, it is useful to be able to describe properties that are only *typical* of a class, and then state that a particular instance of that class is an exception to the rule. Most frame systems allow you to state which properties (ie, slots) are just typical of a class, with exceptions allowed, and which must be true of all instances. The value of a property that is only typical of a class is referred to as a *default* value, and can be *overridden* by giving a different value for an instance or subclass.

The example in Figure 2.4 illustrates this for an extension of our elephant example. Slots preceded by an asterisk (*) hold default values that may be overridden. So, all mammals are warm-blooded but they are only typically furry, and indeed elephants aren't furry. Elephants all have trunks, but are only typically unfurry, grey and large. Clyde is an exception to the rule that elephants are normally grey. He's pink. Nellie is an exception to the rule that elephants are normally large. She's small.

Now, objects and classes inherit the default (typical) properties of their par-

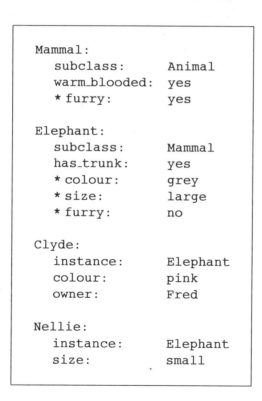

```
Mammal:
    subclass:        Animal
    warm_blooded:    yes
  * furry:           yes

Elephant:
    subclass:        Mammal
    has_trunk:       yes
  * colour:          grey
  * size:            large
  * furry:           no

Clyde:
    instance:        Elephant
    colour:          pink
    owner:           Fred

Nellie:
    instance:        Elephant
    size:            small
```

Figure 2.4 *Elephant Frames with Defaults.*

ent classes UNLESS they have an individual property value that conflicts with the inherited one. Given the above set of frames we can infer that Nellie is warm-blooded, unfurry, has a trunk, grey and small. Clyde is warm-blooded, unfurry, has a trunk, is pink, large and owned by Fred.

Inheritance is simple where each object and class has a single parent class. However, many systems allow *multiple inheritance*, which means that more than one parent class is allowed, and an object or class may inherit from all its parents. This makes inheritance somewhat more complex. Consider the example in Figure 2.5, where Clyde is both an elephant and a circus animal. We can reasonably conclude that Clyde is large and has a trunk (as he's an elephant, and there is no more specific information to contradict this), and that his skills include balancing on a ball (as he's a circus animal). But what can we conclude about his habitat? As he's an elephant it should be the jungle, but as he's a circus animal it should be a tent. A frame system must have some mechanism to decide which value to inherit where there are conflicts like this. One way to do this is to require that the author of the frame system specifies a precedence order for parent classes. For example, by putting Circus-Animal first, this may indicate that where there's a conflict the values should be taken from Circus-Animal rather than from Elephant.

Unfortunately this isn't always sufficient. Suppose there was a slot saying that circus animals were typically small. We now would like to inherit the size property from Elephant, but the habitat property from Circus-animal. There is no easy way to specify this, and it would normally require that an extra class

```
Elephant:
    subclass:       Mammal
    has_trunk:      yes
  * colour:         grey
  * size:           large
  * habitat:        jungle

Circus-Animal:
    subclass:       Animal
    habitat:        tent
    skills:         balancing-on-ball

Clyde:
    instance:       Circus-Animal  Elephant
    colour:         pink
    owner:          Fred
```

Figure 2.5 *Multiple Inheritance.*

`Circus-Elephant` was created, explicitly overriding the `size` and `habitat` properties with the desired values.

2.2.4 Slots and Procedures

In general, both slot values and slots themselves may themselves be frames. In Figure 2.5 Clyde has owner Fred. Fred is the value for the `owner` slot, but might be represented using another frame, so we can describe Fred's properties.

Allowing slots themselves to be frames means that we can specify various attributes of a slot. For example, we could specify that the slot `owner` could only take values of class `person`, has an inverse slot `owns`, and can take `multiple values` (as more than one person can jointly own something).

Many systems allow slots to include *procedures*. The term *procedural attachment* is used for this. An arbitrary piece of program code may be placed in a slot, which is run whenever the value for that slot is needed. We may also allow pieces of code that are run whenever a value is added, perhaps to do consistency checks or to propagate results to other slots.

With all these features, plus multiple inheritance, it may be hard to predict exactly what will be inferred about a given object just by looking at the set of frames. You'd have to know something about how the underi, ng frame system is implemented, such as the order in which things are tried when attempting to determine values of slots. We say that the system has a *procedural* rather than a *declarative* semantics, as the precise meaning of a set of frames depends on how the inferences are done. This is theoretically undesirable, but for practical systems it may be worth sacrificing a clean semantics for additional features and flexibility.

2.2.5 Implementing a Simple Frame System

A basic frame system, that allows default values but not multiple inheritance, can be implemented very simply in any programming language. The frames themselves can be represented using any suitable data structures – we'll just assume that a function `slot-value` has been defined that returns the value for a particular object and attribute if there is a value, or something to indicate that there is no such value. `Slot-value` ignores inheritance.

What we need to define now is a function that will determine what can be inferred by inheritance. A basic algorithm which returns the value for a particular attribute, using inheritance is as follows:

To find `value(O, A)`

- If `slot-value(O, A)` returns a value V, return V.
- Otherwise, if `slot-value(O, subclass)` or `slot-value(O, instance)` returns a value C, find `value(C, A)` and return this value.
- Otherwise, fail.

To see how this works, consider again Figure 2.4. If we wanted to find out Nellie's colour (i.e., `value(Nellie, colour)`) the algorithm would first try `slot-value(Nellie, colour)`. As no specific value is given for Nellie's colour, `slot-value` would indicate that there is no such value, so we try `slot-value(Nellie, subclass)` and `slot-value(Nellie, instance)`. The latter could return `Elephant`, so we call the function recursively and try to find `value(Elephant, colour)`. Now, this time `slot-value(Elephant, colour)` returns `grey`, so this value is returned by `value(Elephant, colour)` and hence also by `value(Nellie, colour)`. Nellie is therefore grey.

2.2.6   Representational Adequacy

Semantic networks and frames provide a fairly simple and clear way of representing properties of objects and categories of objects. A basic type of inference is defined, whereby objects may inherit properties of parent objects.

There are many things that cannot easily be represented using frames. For example, it is hard to express *negation* (i.e., the fact that something is NOT true), *disjunction* (i.e., the fact that either one thing OR another is true), or certain types of *quantification* (i.e., the fact that something is true for ALL or SOME of a set of objects). If these things are needed then using a logic, described next, may be more appropriate. However, frame and semantic network systems still have their place where relatively simple kinds of knowledge need to be represented.

2.3   Predicate Logic

The most important knowledge representation language is arguably predicate logic (or, strictly, first-order predicate logic). Predicate logic allows us to represent fairly complex facts about the world, and to derive new facts in a way that guarantees that, if the initial facts were true, then so are the conclusions. It is a well-understood formal language, with well-defined syntax, semantics and rules of inference. There isn't room in this section to give a full introduction to predicate logic. If you aren't already familiar with the basics you may want to consult an introductory logic text, or introductions in longer AI texts, such as (Ginsberg, 1993) (ch.6); (Russell & Norvig, 1995) (ch.7); (Luger & Stubblefield, 1993) (ch.2). However, a brief summary is given below, which should serve to remind people who have already met predicate logic of the basics, and give those who haven't a flavour of what is involved.

A logic is a formal system which may be described in terms of its *syntax* (what the allowable expressions are), its *semantics* (what they mean) and its *proof theory* (how can we draw new conclusions given some statements in the logic). These three aspects will be briefly discussed first for propositional logic (which is much simpler, but allows the key ideas to be introduced), and then for predicate logic.

2.3.1 Review of Propositional Logic

Syntax

In propositional logic symbols are used to represent facts about the world. For example, the fact "Alison likes cakes" could be represented by the symbol P (or indeed any other symbol, such as the more meaningful $AlisonLikesCakes$). Simple facts like this are referred to as *atomic propositions*. We can build up more complex statements (or *sentences*) by combining atomic propositions with the *logical connectives* ∧ (and) ∨ (or) ¬ (not) → (implication) and ↔ (equivalence). So if we had the proposition Q representing the fact "Alison eats cakes" we could have the facts:

$P \vee Q$: "Alison likes cakes or Alison eats cakes"
$P \wedge Q$: "Alison likes cakes and Alison eats cakes"
$\neg Q$: "Alison doesn't eat cakes"
$P \rightarrow Q$: "If Alison likes cakes then Alison eats cakes".
$P \leftrightarrow Q$: "If Alison likes cakes then Alison eats cakes, and vice versa".

In general, if X and Y are sentences in propositional logic, then so are $X \wedge Y$, $X \vee Y$, $\neg X$, $X \rightarrow Y$, and $X \leftrightarrow Y$. This defines the *syntax* of the logic. The following are all valid sentences in propositional logic:

P ∨¬Q
P ∧ (P → Q)
(Q ∨¬ R) → P

Semantics

The *semantics* of propositional logic allows us to state precisely what statements like those above mean. It is defined in terms of what is true in the world. For example, if we know whether P, Q and R are true, the semantics of the logic will tell you whether sentences such as $(P \vee Q) \wedge R$ are true. (Note that the parentheses are important: $(P \vee Q) \wedge R$ is not the same as $P \vee (Q \wedge R)$.)

We can determine the truth or falsity (or *truth value*) of sentences like these using *truth tables* which define the truth values of sentences with logical connectives in terms of the truth values of their component sentences. The truth tables provide a simple *semantics* for these logical connectives (i.e., define precisely what the logical connectives mean). As sentences can only be true or false, truth tables are very simple, for example:

$X\,Y$	$X \vee Y$
T T	T
T F	T
F T	T
F F	F

From the table above we can see, for example, that if X is true and Y is false then $X \vee Y$ is true. Now, suppose we have an assertion $raining \vee sunny$ – i.e., we state that the truth value of the sentence $raining \vee sunny$ is T. By looking at this truth table we can see that this must mean that either it's raining, or it's sunny, or it's both raining and sunny. So we can work backwards from the truth value of a sentence to find the possible truth values of the constituent propositions – this gives us the meaning of the sentence. Without a precise statement of the semantics of $\vee$ (and the other logical connectives) then the meaning of statements in the logic might be ambiguous. For example, we might decide that $raining \vee sunny$ means that it is either one or the other, but not both.

Proof Theory

In order to infer new facts in a logic we need to apply *inference rules*. The semantics of the logic will define which inference rules are universally *valid*. This gives us the *proof theory* of the logic. One useful inference rule is the following (called *modus ponens*):

$$\frac{A, A \to B}{B}$$

This rule just says that if $A \to B$ is true, and A is true, then B is necessarily true. We could prove that this rule is valid using truth tables. This rule is a *sound* rule of inference for the logic. Given the semantics of the logic, if the premises are true then the conclusions are guaranteed true.

There are many other sound rules of inference. A particularly important one is *resolution*. A simple form of the resolution rule of inference is the following:

$$\frac{A \vee B, \neg B \vee C}{A \vee C}$$

To see how this could be applied, suppose we know that the following two sentences are true:

$$sunny \vee raining$$
$$\neg raining \vee carryumbrella$$

We can use the rule of inference, given the first two sentences, to conclude $sunny \vee carryumbrella$.

If we want to *prove* whether or not a proposition is true, given some sentences that we know are true, the resolution rule of inference is sufficient. First we have to get all the sentences into a standardized or *normal form* that involves sentences like those above. Then there is a procedure called proof by *refutation* that can be applied. The general idea is that we try assuming that the proposition in question is false, and see if that leads to a contradiction.

2.3.2 Predicate Logic

Syntax

The trouble with propositional logic is that it is not possible to write general statements in it, such as "Alison eats everything that she likes". We'd have to have lots of rules, for every different thing that Alison liked. Predicate logic makes such general statements possible.

Sentences in predicate logic are built up from *atomic sentences*. Rather than dealing with undivisible propositions, predicate logic expresses basic facts in terms of a predicate name and some arguments. So, for "Alison likes chocolate" we could have a predicate name *likes*, arguments *alison* and *chocolate* to give the sentence *likes(alison, chocolate)*. This proves much more flexible than just having an indivisible proposition P standing for the whole thing, as we can "get at" the entities *alison*, and *chocolate*.

In general the arguments in an atomic sentence may be any *term*. Terms may be:

Constant symbols such as *alison*.

Variable symbols such as X. For consistency with Prolog we'll use capital letters to denote variables, and avoid capitals for constant symbols.

Function expressions such as *father(alison)*. Function expressions consist of a functor followed by a number of arguments, which can be arbitrary terms.

So, atomic sentences in predicate logic include the following:

- *friends(alison, richard)*
- *friends(father(fred), father(joe))*
- *likes(X, richard)*

Sentences in predicate logic are constructed (much as in propositional logic) by combining atomic sentences with logical connectives, so the following are all sentences in predicate calculus:

- *friends(alison, richard)* → *likes(alison, richard)*
- *likes(alison, richard)* ∨ *likes(alison, chocolate)*
- (*likes(alison, richard)* ∨ *likes(alison, chocolate)*) ∧ ¬*likes(alison, chocolate)*

Sentences can also be formed using *quantifiers* to indicate how any variables in the sentence are to be treated. The two quantifiers in predicate logic are $\forall$ and $\exists$. $\forall$ is read as "for all", and is used to state that something is true for every object, and $\exists$ is read as "there exists", and is used to state that something is true for at least one object. The following are sentences involving quantifiers:

- $\forall X(likes(alison, X) \rightarrow eats(alison, X))$ i.e., Alison eats everything that she likes.
- $\exists X(bird(X) \land \neg flies(X))$ i.e., there exists some bird that doesn't fly.
- $\forall X(person(X) \rightarrow \exists Y loves(X, Y))$ i.e., every person has something that they love.

A sentence should have all its variables quantified. So, strictly, an expression like $\forall X loves(X, Y)$, although a well-formed *formula* of predicate logic, is not a sentence, as the variable Y isn't quantified. Formulae with all their variables quantified are also called *closed formulae*.

Semantics

The semantics of predicate logic is defined (as in propositional logic) in terms of the truth values of sentences. As in propositional logic, we can use truth tables to find the truth value of sentences involving logical connectives from the truth values of each part of the sentence.

However, we also need to deal with predicates, arguments and quantifiers. Formally the meaning of a predicate such as *likes* may be defined in terms of the set of all pairs of people (in some *domain* of interest) that like each other. However, for our purposes we can just assume that, somehow, a truth value can be assigned to a sentence such as *likes(alison, chocolate)*.

The meaning of $\forall$ can be defined in terms of whether some sentence is true for ALL objects in the domain of interest. $\forall X S$ means that for every object X in the domain, S is true. For example, suppose we are only interested in Fred, Jim and Joe. We could work out whether the sentence $\forall X likes(X, chocolate)$ is true by checking, whether $likes(Fred, chocolate)$, $likes(Jim, chocolate)$ and $likes(Joe, chocolate)$ are all true.

The meaning of $\exists$ can be defined similarly, in terms of whether some sentence is true for at least one of the objects in the domain of interest. So, if Fred likes chocolate but the others don't, $\exists X likes(X, chocolate)$ is true, but $\forall X likes(X, chocolate)$ is false. This only gives a flavour of how we can give a semantics to expressions in predicate logic. The details are best left to logicians. The important thing is that everything is very precisely defined, so if we use predicate logic we should know exactly where we are and therefore what inferences are valid.

Proof Theory

Inference rules (and proof procedures) in predicate logic are similar to those for propositional logic. Modus Ponens and Resolution still apply, but have to be

Logic Programming

Logic programming languages view a computer program as a set of statements in logic. Rather than running the program, as you might do in a procedural language, you can give the system statements to try to prove, given the statements in the program. The most widely used logic programming language is Prolog.

Prolog is based on predicate logic. Each statement in the program corresponds to a sentence in predicate logic. However, the notations used are rather different. The following shows a tiny Prolog program and the corresponding statements in logic. Note that all the capitalized arguments in the Prolog have universal quantifiers ($\forall$ signs) in the logic version, and a backwards version of the implication sign, written : - is used in Prolog.

```
father(jim, fred).
father(joe, jim).
grandfather(X, Y) :-
    father(X, Z),
    father(Z, Y).
```

$father(jim, fred)$
$father(joe, jim)$
$\forall XYZ((father(X,\ Z) \wedge father(Z,\ Y)) \rightarrow grandfather(X,\ Y))$

Given the above program we could ask Prolog to prove that `grandfather(joe, fred)` was true. It should answer `yes`. Prolog proves statements using a variant of the resolution procedure outlined in Section 2.3.2. To make things efficient, and to allow a simple and *goal directed* proof procedure, Prolog does not allow arbitrary statements in predicate logic to be represented, but only *horn* clauses where there is just one fact on the right-hand side of an implication sign.

---

modified to deal with expressions which involve variables and quantifiers. For example, we would like to be able to use the facts $\forall X(man(X) \rightarrow mortal(X))$ and $man(socrates)$ and conclude $mortal(socrates)$. To do this we can use modus ponens, but allow sentences to be *matched* with other sentences. For example, $man(X)$ can be matched with $man(socrates)$ with $X = socrates$.

The resolution rule of inference can similarly be modified to work for predicate logic. Proof by refutation can then be applied if we want to try to prove that something is true, given some sentences in the logic. This gives us a *sound* proof procedure – if we prove something using it we can be sure it is a valid conclusion. It is also *complete*, in the sense that it will eventually find a proof, if one exists.

2.3.3   Knowledge Representation using Predicate Logic

Representing Facts in Logic

Your average AI programmer/researcher may not need to know the details of predicate logic semantics or proof theory, but will probably need to know how to represent things in predicate logic, and what expressions in predicate logic mean. Formally we've already gone through what expressions mean, but it may make more sense to give a number of examples, and to outline how you get from a statement expressed in English to a statement in predicate logic.

Statements like "Alison likes chocolate" or "John loves Mary" are easy to express. You just use the verb as the predicate name and the nouns as the arguments, to get $likes(alison, chocolate)$ and $loves(john, mary)$. A statement describing a property of an individual, such as "Mary is tall", can also be easily be expressed, but the convention here is to make this into a one-argument predicate, such as $tall(mary)$. If Mary is both tall and beautiful, the logical connective $\wedge$ must be used: $tall(mary) \wedge beautiful(mary)$. Similarly if Alison likes both chocolate and cream: $likes(alison, chocolate) \wedge likes(alison, cream)$. Note that logical connectives cannot be used within an argument of a predicate, so $likes(alison, chocolate \wedge cream)$ is not correct.

Statements of the form "If X then Y" can be translated into $X \rightarrow Y$. So, "If Alison is hungry then she eats chocolate" could be: $hungry(alison) \rightarrow eats(alison, chocolate)$. For statements involving "or" then the connective $\vee$ may be used: $eats(alison, chocolate) \vee eats(alison, biscuits)$. And to assert that something is not true, $\neg$ is used: $\neg likes(alison, brusselsprouts)$.

For more general rules the quantifier $\forall$ may be used. A common form is $\forall X p(X) \rightarrow q(X)$, where p and q are any predicates. For example, "All students study" could be expressed as $\forall X\ student(X) \rightarrow study(X)$ (that is, for all things, if that thing is a student then that thing will study). The quantifier $\exists$ is used when something only has to be true of one object. For example, "Someone strange likes brussel sprouts" could be expressed as $\exists X\ strange(X) \wedge likes(X, brusselsprouts)$ (i.e., there exists some thing that is both strange and likes brussel sprouts).

The following are some further examples of statements in predicate logic, paired with their English equivalents.

- $\exists X(table(X) \wedge \neg numlegs(X, 4))$ "There is some table that doesn't have 4 legs"
- $\forall X(elephant(X) \rightarrow grey(X))$ "All elephants are grey"
- $\forall X(glaswegian(X) \rightarrow (supports(X, rangers) \vee supports(X, celtic)))$ "All Glaswegians support either Celtic or Rangers"
- $\exists X(small(X) \wedge slimy(X) \wedge on(X, table))$ "There is something small and slimy on the table"
- $\neg\exists X(brusselsprout(X) \wedge tasty(X))$ "There is no brussel sprout which is tasty."

The Use of Logic in AI

Predicate logic provides a powerful way to represent and reason with knowledge. Some things that cannot be easily represented using frames, such as negation, disjunction and quantification, are easily represented using predicate logic. The available inference rules and proof procedures mean that a much wider range of inferences are possible than the simple inheritance-based inference allowed in a frame system.

However, there are some things that are hard to represent using predicate logic, particularly facts that involve uncertainty (e.g., "It will probably rain tomorrow"), defaults (e.g., "It normally rains in Glasgow"), beliefs ("John believes it will rain, but I don't"), and time/change (e.g., "It will get wetter and wetter as you near Glasgow"). Methods have been developed that allow some of these to be handled within predicate logic, and more complex logics have been developed with different syntax and semantics. However, as the logic gets more complex inference within the logic tends to get less efficient. So for complex problem solving the AI programmer might have to choose between a logic-based approach, with clear semantics and guaranteed sound inferences, and a more *ad hoc* procedural approach which might be more efficient for the particular problem.

Within AI, logic is used not just as a knowledge representation language, but also:

- To *communicate* AI theories within the community. When writing about a new theory of human reasoning or language use some people use a formal logic to describe the theory. This adds precision, though sometimes at the expense of clarity and accessibility.
- As the basis of AI *programming languages*. The obvious example here is Prolog, which is based on predicate logic, yet can be used as a flexible and general-purpose AI programming language.
- To give the meaning of natural language sentences in a natural language understanding system.
- To define the *semantics* of other simpler representation languages. This is discussed in more detail below.

Logic and Frames

Representation languages such as frames often have their semantics defined in terms of predicate (or other) logics. Once we have defined precisely what all the expressions and relations mean in terms of a well-understood logic then we can make sure than any inferences that are drawn are sound, according to that logic. For a simple frame system, without defaults, one way to translate things into logic is as follows:

- For an object o with slot s and value v we get: $\forall X \exists Y (o(X) \rightarrow (v(Y) \wedge s(X,Y)))$. For example, for our "Elephant has_part head" example from Section 2.2.1 we'd get the translation as: $\forall X \exists Y (elephant(X) \rightarrow head(Y) \wedge haspart(X,Y))$.

- If one object o is an instance of a class c we get: $c(o)$. For example, Nellie's an elephant: $elephant(nellie)$.
- If one class $c1$ is a subclass of another class $c2$ we get: $\forall X(c1(X) \rightarrow c2(X))$. For example: $\forall X elephant(X) \rightarrow mammal(X)$.

Inheritance still works in the logic-based version. For example, the inference rule modus ponens could be applied to $\forall X \exists Y(elephant(X) \rightarrow head(Y) \wedge haspart(X, \ Y))$ and $elephant(nellie)$ to conclude that $\exists Y head(Y) \wedge haspart(nellie, \ Y)$ (i.e., Nellie has a head).

Using this model everything in a frame system can be translated into predicate logic, but not vice versa. The frame system has weaker *representational adequacy*. However, the frame system is easy to work with, and being able to translate between frames and logic has the advantage that we can deal (on the surface) with a simple, natural representation language such as frames, while underneath we can be confident that the inferences drawn by the system are all sound. Of course, we have to understand something about the semantics of the language to be able to represent things meaningfully in it, but this may not be as awkward as dealing directly with the logic.

Another possible advantage of this approach is that something like a frame system typically has restricted representational power compared with full predicate (or default) logic. This may sound like a disadvantage, as it will mean there are some things we can't represent. However, the gain in efficiency by reasoning with a restricted subset usually makes this tradeoff worthwhile. In fact, new logics (called *terminological* or *description* logics) have been developed, which have the expressive power needed to perform inheritance type inferences on simple properties of classes of objects (as in frame systems), but which do not allow some of inferences and representations possible in predicate logic. These allow you to reason directly in the logic, rather than using the special inferences of a frame system, which are only indirectly validated by a logic-based semantics. Terminological logics have more restricted expressive power than predicate logic, but greater efficiency.

2.3.4 Conclusion

This section has just given a quick overview of predicate logic and its use in knowledge representation. Although it is more powerful as a language than, say, frames, some facts may be less clear when represented using a logic. For example, for most people the "Elephant has_part head" example is more natural and easier to understand in the frame or semantic network-based representation. And although predicate logic allows a wide range of inferences, and there are proof procedures that can be used to apply these inferences in a systematic way, the process may be inefficient when compared with a more restricted language such as frames. There is a tradeoff between representational and inferential adequacy (i.e., the expressiveness of the system) and inferential efficiency.

Although logic is not a panacea as a knowledge representation language, it is more fundamental than the other methods described in this chapter, as other methods are often described in terms of logic. Logic provides a firm foundation on which other methods can stand, allowing them to be analysed and compared. More advanced study of AI would require a closer examination of the role of logic.

2.4   Rule-Based Systems

Instead of representing knowledge in a relatively declarative, static way (as a set of things that are true), rule-based systems represent knowledge in terms of a set of rules that tell you what you should do or what you can conclude in different situations. A rule-based system consists of a set of IF–THEN rules, a set of *facts* normally representing things that are currently held to be true, and some *interpreter* controlling the application of the rules, given the facts. This is illustrated in Figure 2.6.

The IF–THEN rules in a rule-based system are treated very differently from similar constructs in a conventional programming language such as Pascal or C. While Pascal or C treats IF–THEN constructs as part of a *sequence* of instructions, to be considered in order, a rule-based system treats each rule as an independent chunk of knowledge, to be invoked when needed under the control of the interpreter. The rules are more like implications in logic (e.g., $raining \rightarrow carry\_umbrella$), and indeed the discussion of forward and backward chaining below applies equally well to the control of reasoning in a logic-based system.

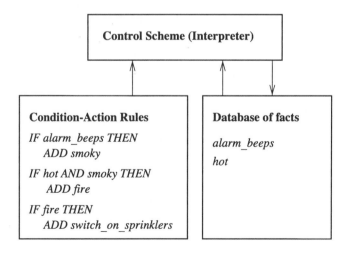

Figure 2.6 *Rule-Based System Architecture.*

There are two main kinds of interpreter: *forward chaining* and *backward chaining*. In a forward chaining system you start with some initial facts, and keep using the rules to draw new conclusions (or take certain actions) given those facts. In a backward chaining system you start with some hypothesis (or goal) you are trying to prove, and keep looking for rules that would allow you to conclude that hypothesis, perhaps setting new subgoals to prove as you go. Forward chaining systems are primarily data-driven, while backward chaining systems are goal-driven. We'll look at both, and when each might be useful.

2.4.1   Forward Chaining Systems

In a forward chaining system the facts in the system are held in a *working memory* which is continually updated as rules are invoked. Rules in the system represent possible actions to take when specified facts occur in the working memory, and are often referred to as *condition-action rules*. The actions usually involve *adding* or *deleting* items from the working memory, but other actions are possible, such as printing a message. Indeed, many systems may allow arbitrary procedures to be called within the action part of the rule.

The interpreter controls the application of the rules, given the working memory, thus controlling the system's activity. It is based on a cycle of activity sometimes known as a *recognize–act* cycle. The system first checks to find all the rules whose conditions hold, given the current state of working memory. It then selects one and performs the actions in the action part of the rule. This is referred to as *firing* the rule. The selection of a rule to fire is based on fixed strategies, known as *conflict resolution* strategies, discussed later. Anyway, the actions will result in a new working memory, and the cycle begins again. This cycle will be repeated until either no rules fire, or a special *halt* symbol is added to working memory.

This basic algorithm for forward chaining may be summarized as follows:

Repeat:

- Find all the rules which have conditions (IF part) satisfied.
- Select one, using conflict resolution strategies.
- Perform actions in conclusion, possibly modifying current working memory.

until no rules can fire or *halt* in working memory.

A Simple Example

As a very simple illustration, consider the rules and facts in Figure 2.6, which capture a rather conservative approach to fire fighting (only switch the sprinklers on if the smoke alarm goes off AND it's hot – you don't want to make the burnt toast wet):

R1: *IF hot AND smoky THEN ADD fire*
R2: *IF alarm_beeps THEN ADD smoky*

R3: *IF fire THEN ADD switch_on_sprinklers*
F1: *alarm_beeps*
F2: *hot*

Initially the system checks to find the rules whose conditions hold, given the two facts (F1 and F2). The only such rule is rule R2, so this rule is selected and its action is performed. The action *ADD smoky* is an instruction to add a new fact *smoky* to the working memory. So a new fact is added:

F3: *smoky*

Now the cycle starts again. 1   , time the conditions of the first rule hold, as both *hot* and *smoky* are in the working memory. So the action is performed, and we get a new fact in working memory:

F4: *fire*

The cycle begins again, and this time rule R3 fires, *switch_on_sprinklers* is added to working memory, and hopefully as a result the sprinklers switched on!

This example at least illustrates how the order in which rules fires depends on what is in working memory and not on the order in which the rules are given. However, what happens if, in some cycle, more than one rule has its condition satisfied? To discuss this we'll extend the above example a little, with two more rules and one new initial fact:

R1: *IF hot AND smoky THEN ADD fire*
R2: *IF alarm_beeps THEN ADD smoky*
R3: *IF fire THEN ADD switch_on_sprinklers*
R4: *IF dry THEN ADD switch_on_humidifier*
R5: *IF sprinklers_on THEN DELETE dry*
F1: *alarm_beeps*
F2: *hot*
F3: *dry*

The action *DELETE dry* will result in this fact being removed from working memory. Now, in the first cycle there are TWO rules that apply: R2 and R4. If R4 is chosen, the humidifier is switched on and then things proceed as before. If R2 is chosen, followed by R1, R3 and R4, then *dry* is deleted from working memory and the humidifier (sensibly) never switched on.

Conflict Resolution

Clearly it is important which rule is chosen to fire when there is a choice. This may influence the final conclusions, as we have seen, and also the efficiency of the system in arriving at the conclusion or action of interest (without drawing too many irrelevant conclusions or doing too many irrelevant actions along the way). A forward chaining system will have some *conflict resolution strategies* to decide which rules to fire. Common strategies include:

- prefer to fire rules that involve facts that have been recently added to working memory. In the above example, if initially R2 fires, the next rule to fire will be R1 (rather than R4) as *smoky* has been recently added. This allows the system to follow through a single chain of reasoning.
- prefer to fire rules with more specific conditions. For example, if we had a rule R6: *IF hot THEN ADD summer*, and facts *hot* and *smoky*, R1 would be fired in preference to R6 as it has more specific conditions. This allows you to have rules like R1 which are exceptions to a more general rule (R6).
- allow user to prioritize rules. For example, R4 above could have very low priority, only fired if nothing else can fire.
- fire all applicable rules at once. This is pretty much the opposite of the first strategy listed, as it results in all chains of reasoning being explored simultaneously. (This is similar to the difference between *depth first* and *breadth first* search strategies discussed in Chapter 4.)

A forward chaining language may provide a range of different strategies for the person writing the rules to select between.

Reason Maintenance

Another feature that is sometimes offered is for the system to automatically withdraw facts whose *justifications* have become invalidated because of changes in the working memory. In the fire example above, the humidifier could be switched on (or at least *switch_on_humidifier* added), with the justification that it is hot and dry. But later *dry* is removed from the working memory, so *switch_on_humidifier* no longer has a valid justification, so could be automatically removed.

Sophisticated techniques have been developed to allow these sorts of updates, referred to as *reason maintenance* or *truth maintenance* systems. Some allow all possible consistent sets of facts to be considered. For example, suppose (for some reason) that the sprinkler system should not be switched on if the humidifier is on. There would be two consistent sets of facts, one with the humidifier on (and the building burning down!) and one with the sprinkler on.

Pattern Matching

The rules and facts in the examples so far have been very simple. In general more complex facts are allowed, such as *temperature(kitchen, hot)* rather than just *hot*, and rules can have *patterns* that are *matched* against facts in the working memory. For example, suppose we have the following rule and facts:

> R7: *IF temperature(R, hot) AND environment(R, smoky) then ADD fire_in(R)*
> F6: *temperature(kitchen, hot)*
> F7: *environment(kitchen, smoky)*

The rule conditions contain a variable R which may take any value (e.g., kitchen)[5].

---

[5]Prolog-like notation is used here, for those familiar with Prolog. However, other notations are

The CLIPS Expert System Tool

One expert system tool based on a forward chaining is CLIPS (standing for C Language Integrated Production System). The following rule gives an idea of how you'd write rules using the CLIPS syntax. *Assert* is used rather than *ADD*, and the symbol $=>$ rather than *IF ... THEN*. Variables in patterns are indicated by a question mark.

```
(defrule fire-alarm
  (temperature ?r1 hot)
  (environment ?r1 smoky)
  =>
  (assert (fire-in ?r1)))
```

CLIPS allows a variety of conflict resolution strategies to be selected, and provides limited facilities for reason maintenance. It also provides facilities where rule-based programming may be combined with more conventional procedural and object-based approaches.

CLIPS is fairly widely used, particularly within universities for teaching and research, but also by commercial companies.

So *temperature(R, hot)* matches *temperature(kitchen, hot)* with *R=kitchen*. *Environment(R, kitchen)* (with R=kitchen) matches F7, so the fact *fire_in(kitchen)* is added to the working memory.

For backward chaining (discussed in the next section) pattern matching is used to match goals to conclusions of rules. So if we were trying to prove *fire_in(library)* this goal would match rule R7's conclusion with *R=library*.

Allowing patterns and pattern matching greatly increases the flexibility of rules, whether using forward or backward chaining.

2.4.2 Backward Chaining Systems

So far we have looked at how rule-based systems can be used to draw new conclusions from existing data, adding these conclusions to a working memory. This approach is most useful when you know all the initial facts, but don't know what conclusions are likely.

If you DO know what the conclusion might be, or have some specific hypothesis to test, forward chaining systems may be inefficient. You could keep on forward chaining until either no more rules apply or you have added your hypothesis to the

---

often used for patterns, such as *(temperature ?R hot)*.

working memory. But in the process the system is likely to do a lot of irrelevant work, adding uninteresting conclusions to working memory. For example, suppose we have the following rules (modifying our example again to illustrate a point):

R1: *IF smoky AND hot THEN ADD fire*
R2: *IF alarm_beeps THEN ADD smoky*
R3: *IF alarm_beeps THEN ADD ear_plugs*
R4: *IF fire THEN ADD switch_on_sprinklers*
R5: *IF smoky THEN ADD poor_visibility*
F1: *alarm_beeps*
F2: *hot*

If we are only interested in whether or not to switch on the sprinklers, then concluding that visibility is poor and that you should wear your ear plugs is irrelevant (if not downright dangerous).

By backward chaining we avoid drawing these irrelevant inferences, and focus just on the hypothesis in question (should the sprinklers be switched on?). We start with a goal to try to prove, say, *switch_on_sprinklers*. The system will then check whether the goal matches any of the facts given. If it does, then that goal succeeds. If it doesn't the system will look for rules whose conclusions (previously referred to as *actions*) match the goal. One such rule will be chosen, and the system will then try to prove any facts in the conditions (or *preconditions*) of the rule using the same procedure, setting these as new goals to prove. Note that a backward chaining system does not need to update a working memory. Instead it needs to keep track of what goals it needs to prove in order to prove its main hypothesis.

The following gives the basic algorithm (though ignores the issue of what to do if there is more than one rule that can be used to conclude a given goal):

To prove goal G:

- If G is in the initial facts it is proven.

- Otherwise, find a rule which can be used to conclude G, and try to prove each of that rule's preconditions. G is then proved true if all the preconditions are proved true.

2.4.3   Example

For the example rules above initially the goal to try to prove is:

G1: *switch_on_sprinklers*

We check whether the goal state is in the initial facts. As it isn't there, we try matching it against the conclusions of the rules. It matches rule R4. The precondition of

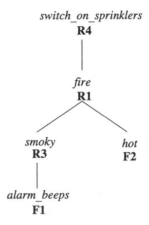

Figure 2.7 *Proof Tree for Sprinkler Example.*

this rule is set as a new goal to prove:

G2: *fire*

Now, this isn't in the facts, but it matches the conclusion of rule R1, so R1's preconditions are set as new goals to prove:

G3: *smoky*
G4: *hot*

G3 is considered first. It matches the conclusion of R2, so *alarm_beeps* is set as a new goal. The goals to prove are now:

G5: *alarm_beeps*
G4: *hot*

Now, both of these are in the initial facts, so are trivially true. As all the goals are now proved, the initial goal must be true, so we can conclude that the sprinkler should be switched on.

The proof for our hypothesis *switch_on_sprinklers* can be represented graphically as a tree, illustrated in Figure 2.7.

2.4.4 Implementation

A backward chaining system may be implemented using a stack to record the goals that are still to be satisfied[6]. You repeatedly pop a goal off the stack, and try and prove it. If it is in the set of initial facts then it is proved. If it matches a rule which

---

[6]A simple recursive implementation is also possible, but less easy to modify if you want to try different *search strategies*. See chapter 4.

has a number of preconditions then the preconditions are pushed onto the stack. Otherwise the goal fails. The overall goal succeeds if all subgoals are successfully removed from the stack, and none fails.

However, what should be done if there is more than one rule that has the same conclusion, and could be used to prove a particular goal? In this case the system should try them all, and see if the goal can be proved using *any* of them. *Search techniques*, discussed in Chapter 4, may be used to try all the possibilities in this way. For example, using a *depth first search* algorithm, if it fails to prove a goal using one rule it will "back up" to the last point where there was a choice of rules and try the alternative.

The Prolog language uses backward chaining with depth first search to try to prove things, and has built-in *pattern matching* facilities. This makes it a good choice for prototyping simple expert systems. Usually you'd first write an expert system *shell* (or special-purpose language) using Prolog, then write the expert system itself using that shell. This has the advantage that you can choose the notation to be used for your rules, and can program in extra features that aren't directly supported in Prolog. Such features might include methods for handling uncertainty or interacting with the user. These are discussed more in the next chapter.

Forwards vs Backwards Reasoning

Whether you use forward or backwards reasoning to solve a problem depends on the properties of your rule set and initial facts, and on how many possible hypotheses there are to consider. If you have some particular hypothesis to test, then backward chaining may be more efficient, as you avoid drawing conclusions from irrelevant facts. However, sometimes backward chaining can be very wasteful – there may be many possible hypotheses, and for each one there may be many ways to try to prove it, few of which result in a conclusion.

Consider, for example, two applications of expert systems mentioned in Chapter 1. For medical diagnosis, in a very restricted area, there may only be, say, ten diseases of interest. It would be practical to use backward chaining and try and prove each one in turn, and indeed a pioneering expert system MYCIN (discussed further in the next chapter) does just this. However, for an application like computer configuration there are an enormous number of possible configurations, and it would not be sensible to go through all the possibilities until one was found meeting the customer's specifications. For this application forward chaining is a better idea, starting with the specifications and gradually building up (in working memory) a possible configuration. Another pioneering system XCON did just this. This was a system to configure VAX computer systems, and was one of the early commercial successes of expert system technology.

2.5 Comparing Knowledge Representation Languages

So far we have discussed three approaches to knowledge representation and inference: frames and semantic networks, logic, and rules. Logic is the most fundamental of these, and other methods may sometimes be described in terms of logic.

Frames and networks are useful for representing declarative information about collections of related objects/concepts, and in particular where there is a clear *class hierarchy*, and where you want to use *inheritance* to infer the attributes of objects in subclasses from the attributes of objects in the parent class. Early approaches tended to have poorly specified *semantics* but there are now practical systems with a clear underlying semantics. Logic is generally used to describe this semantics.

Frames and networks are unlikely to be adequate if you want to draw a wide range of different sorts of inferences, and not just inferences based on inheritance. For this you could use the full power of predicate logic, along with a theorem prover. Logic-based approaches allow you to represent fairly complex things (involving quantification, negation and disjunction), and have a well-defined syntax, semantics and proof theory. However, logic-based approaches may be inflexible. Any inference rules in the logic must be validated by a precisely stated semantics for expressions in the language. This may mean that many commonsense inferences and conclusions aren't allowed, and reasoning may be inefficient.

Rule-based systems provide more flexibility, sometimes allowing arbitrary procedures within the rules. More emphasis may be placed on how the reasoning is controlled, but the semantics of the rules may be unspecified – the conclusions drawn by the system just depend on details of how the the rule interpreter works. While logic is used in a declarative way, saying what's true in the world, rule-based systems (especially forward chaining systems) are concerned more with procedural knowledge – what to do when.

A common feature of all the approaches is that the problem-specific rules and facts are represented separately from the more general problem-solving and inference procedures used to reason with these. It should be possible to modify a system, or write a system to solve a related problem, without ever modifying the problem-solving or inference methods. We just add, for example, new rules, frames, or statements in a logic, re-using both existing facts and tried-and-tested problem-solving and inference methods. A knowledge representation language provides us with representational notations and inference methods that have both been found to be useful, and which have been analysed to make sure that they are sound. Using such a language for AI problem solving therefore provides significant advantages over, say, writing a C++ program from scratch, where the programmer has to re-invent suitable notations and do all the hard work of checking the correctness of the methods herself.

2.6   Summary

- Knowledge representation languages provide high-level representation formalisms to represent the knowledge required for AI problem solving.
- A good language should be natural, clear and precise, allow you to represent what is required, and support the sound inference of new facts.
- Frames and semantic networks represent knowledge as an organized collection of objects with attributes, arranged in a hierarchy. If an object is a *subclass* of another it may inherit its attributes. They are limited in what can be represented and inferred, but provide a natural and efficient representation scheme.
- A logic, and in particular predicate logic, may be used as a precise and formal language able to represent a fairly wide range of things. A logic may also be used to describe the semantics of other formalisms.
- Rule-based systems allow knowledge to be represented as a set of more-or-less independent IF–THEN or condition-action rules, stating what action to take given different conditions. Reasoning can be controlled using a *forward* or *backward* chaining interpreter.

2.7   Further Reading

Most recent AI textbooks have emphasized logic-based approaches to knowledge representation. Ginsberg (Ginsberg, 1993) (ch.6–9) gives a good introduction to the use of logic, with a briefer discussion of frames and nets (ch.13), building on the discussion of logic. Russell & Norvig (Russell & Norvig, 1995) (ch.6–10) provide a more advanced treatment of logic, but very little discussion of rules or frames. Rich & Knight (Rich & Knight, 1991) (ch.4–11) give a good discussion of all the topics, with more discursive material and advanced topics. Luger and Stubblefield (Luger & Stubblefield, 1993) (ch.2,8,9) also cover most of the material, although organised rather differently.

Further information about AI and Prolog can be found in (Pereira & Shieber, 1987) (which, although emphasizing natural language applications, includes a good discussion of the proof procedure and resolution) and (Bratko, 1990).

2.8   Exercises

1. Represent the following facts as a set of frames:
   "The aorta is a particular kind of artery which has a diameter of 2.5 cm. An artery is a kind of blood vessel. An artery always has a muscular wall, and

generally has a diameter of 0.4 cm. A vein is a kind of blood vessel, but has a fibrous wall. Blood vessels all have tubular form and contain blood."

2. Represent the following facts in the language of predicate logic:

   - Every apple is either green or yellow.
   - No apple is blue.
   - If an apple is green then it is tasty.
   - Every man likes a tasty apple.

3. "Herbert is a small hippopotamus who lives in Edinburgh zoo. Like all hippopotamuses he eats grass and likes swimming"
   Represent the above:

   (a) as a semantic network;

   (b) in predicate logic.

   Give two new facts about Herbert that are:

   (a) easier to represent in a semantic network than in predicate logic;

   (b) easier to represent in logic than in a semantic network.

4. Give a set of frames representing facts about students in general, students at your university, and students on your course, making good use of inheritance, and indicating which slots hold default values.

5. The following IF–THEN rules are proposed for a simple rule-based financial advice expert system:

   R1: *IF NOT savings_adequate THEN ADD invest_savings*

   R2: *IF savings_adequate AND income_adequate THEN ADD invest_stocks*

   R3: *IF NOT has_children THEN ADD savings_adequate*

   R4: *IF has_partner AND partner_has_job THEN ADD income_adequate*

   (a) For the hypothesis *invest_stocks* outline how this could be proved through backward chaining. Assume that current facts include: *has_children, has_partner* and *partner_has_job*.

   (b) Currently if you have a partner who works the system concludes that your income is adequate, even if she/he works in the chip shop and you have 15 kids to support. Also if you do not have kids it concludes that your savings are adequate even if you don't have any and want to buy a house. Finally it ignores the fact that if you have a really huge income then these may be adequate even if you have kids and your partner does not work. Extend the rule set to deal with these issues.

CHAPTER 3

Expert Systems

Aims:	To introduce the basics of expert system architecture and development, with case studies in medicine illustrating different approaches.
Objectives:	You should be able to: Describe the basic architecture of an expert system. Discuss whether a given problem could be solved using an expert systems approach and outline how expert systems are typically developed. Describe in detail the operation of a simple backward chaining expert system and be able to design and implement such a system given an English description of the problem and underlying knowledge. Outline different methods for reasoning under uncertainty. Describe and compare three approaches used in medical expert systems.
Prerequisites:	Chapter 2. Also, some basic understanding of probability may be helpful.

3.1 Introduction

So far we have talked a lot about how we can represent knowledge, but not so much about how we can use it to solve real practical problems. This section will therefore look at how some of the techniques discussed so far are used in *expert systems* – systems which provide expert quality advice, diagnoses and recommendations given real world problems.

Expert systems solve real problems which normally would require a human expert (such as a specialist doctor or a minerologist). The human expertise may be in short supply, expensive, and experts hard to get hold of in a hurry. An expert system, on the other hand, may be made easily available on demand. An example situation where we might want to consider using an expert system is in diagnosing rare diseases. A general practitioner may not have the specialized expertise required, human experts may be hard to get hold of in a hurry, yet fast decisions may be required on treatment.

Building an expert system first involves extracting the relevant knowledge from the human expert. Such knowledge is often *heuristic* in nature, based on useful "rules of thumb" rather than absolute certainties. Extracting it from the expert in a way that can be used by a computer is generally a difficult task, requiring its own expertise. A *knowledge engineer* has the job of extracting this knowledge and building the expert system *knowledge base*.

A first attempt at building an expert system is unlikely to be very successful. This is partly because the expert generally finds it very difficult to express exactly what knowledge and rules they use to solve a problem. Much of it is almost subconscious, or appears so obvious they don't even bother mentioning it. *Knowledge acquisition* for expert systems is a major part of expert system design, with a wide variety of techniques used. However, generally this will involve interviewing the expert and getting them to solve a range of typical problems. An initial prototype may be developed based on that, and shown to the expert. The expert may then check the system's performance and give feedback to enable the design to be refined. This may be repeated until the expert is happy. Of course, it is not just the domain expert that has to be happy with a system – the end users of the system and the person (or organization) ordering the system must also be considered, and feedback should be sought from them at each stage.

In order to do such iterative development from a prototype it is important that the expert system is written in a way that it can easily be inspected and modified. The system should be able to explain its reasoning (to expert, user and knowledge engineer) and answer questions about the solution process. Updating the system shouldn't involve rewriting a whole lot of code – just adding or deleting localized chunks of knowledge.

A widely used approach for representing knowledge in an an expert systems is the use of IF–THEN rules (as discussed in Chapter 2) sometimes in combination with frames. Often the rules won't have certain conclusions – there will just be some degree of certainty that the conclusion will hold if the conditions hold. Methods are required to determine the certainty of the overall conclusion given the evidence and these uncertain rules. Rule-based systems, with or without certainties, are flexible, moderately easily modifiable and make it easy to provide reasonably helpful traces of the system's reasoning. These traces can be used in providing explanations of what the system is doing.

Expert systems have been used to solve a wide range of problems in domains such as medicine, mathematics, engineering, geology, computer science, business, law, defence and education. Within each domain, they have been used to solve different types of problems. So, in electronics one type of problem might involve *diagnosing* faults in circuits, another might involve *designing* a circuit to do a particular job. What is generally found is that the appropriate problem-solving methods to use for a given problem depend more on the type of problem than on the application domain. So, diagnosing a fault in a circuit is, in some ways, more like diagnosing a disease than designing a circuit, while designing a circuit might have more in common with designing a kitchen! Of course, both circuit problems will have in common a need for information about, say, circuit components, but representing this knowledge tends to be relatively easy – the hard part is working out a good method to use to solve the problem.

There is a huge range of problem-solving methods that have been used for different expert system tasks. Designing an expert system depends on being able to pick out a good method, and whole books have been written on how this can be done more reliably. However, in this chapter we will mainly discuss the task of *diagnosis*, and consider just three problem-solving techniques that can be used for this problem, focusing most on a rule-based approach using backward chaining.

In the rest of this chapter we will first describe in general terms how an expert system is developed, then talk in more detail about simple backward chaining systems, discuss the problem of how to deal with *uncertainty* in an expert system, and conclude by looking at three contrasting systems which illustrate different techniques that have been used for developing systems for performing diagnosis in medicine.

3.2   Designing an Expert System

Expert systems are extremely diverse in the problems tackled and the detailed problem-solving methods used. However, there are common issues relevant to the design of all systems. These concern the type of problems that are considered suitable for expert systems, the way a system is (typically) developed, and the overall architecture that is commonly used. This section will discuss these general issues.

3.2.1   Choosing a Problem

Writing an expert system generally involves a great deal of time and money. To avoid costly and embarrassing failures, people have developed a set of guidelines to determine whether a problem is suitable for an expert system solution.

First, as with any software engineering project, it is important to be realistic about the costs involved and ensure that the expense is justified given expected benefits. It is easy to underestimate the effort and cost of developing a full-scale expert system, particularly after exploring the basic ideas through simple examples. Even with sophisticated tools now available to aid the development process, it is still a complex process, partly because of the difficulties of acquiring the knowledge from human experts, and the inevitable need to keep going back to expert(s), users, and customer. The costs may be justified where human expertise is in short supply, or not always available when needed. For example, highly specialized medical knowledge may be hard to obtain on demand, but a (non-specialized) doctor must be able make a quick decision about what immediate actions to take, and whether to refer a patient to an expensive and distant specialist.

Second, we must ensure that expert system techniques are appropriate. Problems that require manual dexterity or physical skill are unlikely to be appropriate, even with the advance of techniques in robotics. Also, problems that require a lot of common-sense knowledge probably won't be appropriate, as common sense is notoriously hard to capture and represent. Generally highly technical fields are easier to deal with, as they involve relatively small amounts of well-formalized knowledge, often largely captured in written documents (e.g., medical texts). Typically a suitable problem for an expert system is one that requires highly specialized expertise, but which would only take a human expert a short time to solve (say an hour, maximum).

For some problems using expert system techniques would be an overkill. It may be that you can sketch a relatively simple flowchart (or similar) giving the right expert decision for different situations, and then encode this as a simple program. Flowcharts are sometimes used, for example, to help people make decisions about how to invest their money. A computer implementation of such a flowchart would not need complex techniques. Alternatively, it may be that simple methods based on probability theory can be used, and a spreadsheet used to implement the system. (This latter approach is discussed further in Section 3.4.) You might still choose to refer to the resulting system as an expert system (as it might give useful expert advice), but the methods used are quite simple. If simple methods will do, don't bother looking for a complex solution!

Finally, if we have established that there is a need for an expert system, and that expert system techniques are appropriate and feasible, we need to check that the situation is right for expert system development. Particularly, it is important that there are available and cooperative experts who can contribute their expertise without feeling that the system might make them redundant. You also need any management and potential users to be involved and have positive attitudes to the project.

Only a fairly small range of problems are appropriate for expert system technology. However, given a suitable problem, expert systems can bring great benefits. Systems have been developed, for example, to help analyse samples collected in oil exploration, and to help configure computer systems. Both these systems were successful and in active use.

3.2.2 Knowledge Engineering

Having decided that your problem is suitable you need to extract the knowledge from the expert and represent it using some suitable knowledge representation scheme. This is the job of the *knowledge engineer*, but involves close collaboration with the *expert(s)* and the *end user(s)*.

The knowledge engineer knows about expert system problem-solving and knowledge representation methods, and how to get the domain expert to express their expertise in a usable form. He/she should be able to extract the knowledge from the expert (without thumbscrews!), select appropriate representation and problem-solving methods, and represent the knowledge and methods using suitable tools.

The knowledge engineer may initially have no knowledge of the expert's field. However, to extract knowledge from the expert the knowledge engineer must first become at least somewhat familiar with the area, maybe by reading introductory texts or talking to the expert. After this, more systematic interviewing of the expert begins. Typically experts are set a series of example problems, and will explain aloud their reasoning in solving the problem. The knowledge engineer will abstract general rules from these explanations, and check them with the expert.

As in most applications, the system is wasted if the user is not happy with it, so development must involve close collaboration with potential users. As mentioned in the introduction, the basic development cycle should involve the rapid development of an initial prototype and iterative testing and modification of that prototype with both experts (to check the validity of the expert knowledge) and users (to check that they can provide the necessary information to the system, are satisfied with the systems performance, and that it actually makes their life easier rather than harder!).

In order to develop the initial prototype the knowledge engineer must make provisional decisions about appropriate knowledge representation and inference methods (e.g., rules, or rules in conjunction with frames; forward chaining or backward chaining). To test these basic design decisions, the first prototype may only solve a small part of the overall problem. If the methods used seem to work well for that small part it may be worth investing the effort in representing the rest of the knowledge in the same form.

3.2.3   Expert System Architecture

While the details of an expert system may vary widely, most have a similar overall architecture. The whole system involves much more than just the knowledge base, but will normally involve further components or modules as illustrated in Figure 3.1.

The user interacts with the system through a *user interface* which may use menus, natural language or any other style of interaction. Then an *inference engine* (or problem-solving component) is used to reason with both the *expert knowledge* in the knowledge base and data specific to the particular problem being solved. This *case-specific data* includes both data provided by the user and partial conclusions based on this data.

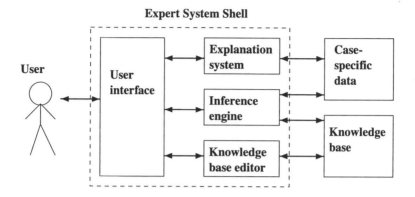

Figure 3.1 *Expert System Architecture.*

As an example, consider a very simple expert system to diagnose colds and 'flu. We might use a *backward chaining* inference engine, using expert knowledge encoded as rules (e.g., IF symptom(Person, runny_nose) THEN disease(Person, cold)). Case-specific data might include facts like symptom(fred, runny_nose).

Most expert systems also have an *explanation subsystem*, which allows the program to explain its reasoning to the user. Some systems also have a *knowledge base editor* which helps the expert or knowledge engineer to easily update and check the knowledge base.

One important feature of expert systems is the way they (usually) separate domain (problem area) specific knowledge from more general-purpose reasoning and representation techniques. The general-purpose part (in the dotted box in the figure) can often be re-used for different problems, and is referred to as an *expert system shell* or *toolkit*. As we see in the figure, the shell will provide the inference engine (and knowledge representation scheme), a user interface, an explanation system and sometimes a knowledge base editor. Given a new kind of problem to solve (say, car design), we can often find a shell that provides the right sort of support for that problem, so all we need to do is provide the expert knowledge. There are numerous commercial expert system shells, each one appropriate for a slightly different range of problems. Using shells to write expert systems generally greatly reduces the cost and time of development (compared with writing the expert system from scratch). One freely available shell is CLIPS (mentioned in Chapter 2), which is primarily a forward chaining system, but allows the users to define *objects*, write functions, and interface easily to programs written in other languages[1].

---

[1]See WWW page (*http://www.cee.hw.ac.uk/ ̃alison/essence.html*) for details of how to obtain CLIPS.

3.2.4   Problem-Solving Methods

In the discussion above we have talked about the selection of an appropriate problem-solving method. Here we'll very briefly consider what these might be like and why they are needed.

A simple expert system might consist of some facts about the current problem (e.g., `symptom(patient1, cough)`), and some inference rules (e.g., `IF symptom(P, cough) THEN ADD disease(P, cold)`). The inference rules would state what can be concluded from the current facts. We can think of an expert system problem-solving method as a way of controlling these inferences so that just those inferences that are required for the current problem are made. If inferences were made at random then a lot of unnecessary work would be done.

This is particularly important if the system might have to ask the user questions in order to elicit more case-specific data (e.g., "Does the patient have a sore throat?"). If the inferences aren't controlled in a sensible manner then the user might be asked irrelevant questions (e.g., "Does the patient have a sore ankle?" after finding that they have a cough).

The forward chaining and backward chaining methods described in the previous chapter provide basic general-purpose methods of controlling inference. And indeed, a backward chaining method can be used fairly directly as the problem-solving strategy for a simple expert system, as we'll see in the next section. However, very often more complex strategies are required, or at least desirable. For example, in medicine a technique called *differential diagnosis* is often used by human experts – this basically involves having a set of current hypotheses about the patient's disease, and trying to ask questions to differentiate between the most likely current hypotheses. These higher-level problem-solving strategies many be implemented in a variety of ways. For example, a forward chaining rule interpreter can be used to implement a differential diagnosis problem-solving strategy, but other underlying methods may also be used. Often, rules in a rule-based expert system may be split into a small number of rules that are concerned with implementing the problem-solving strategy, and a larger number that contain the basic inferences in the problem domain. For example, in medicine we might have problem-solving rules such as `IF too_many_hypotheses THEN rule_out_hypothesis`, and domain rules such as `IF symptom(Patient, cough) THEN disease_hypothesis(Patient, cold)`.

The next section will discuss a very simple problem-solving strategy based on backward chaining. However, the case studies in Section 3.5 will illustrate some contrasting strategies, all for the same problem of medical diagnosis. The first is based largely on simple backward chaining, with *certainty factors* to handle uncertainty. The next uses a more complex problem-solving method based on differential diagnosis. The final one uses methods based on probability and decision theory.

3.3 Backward Chaining Rule-Based Expert Systems

In this section we will show how simple expert systems based on IF–THEN rules and a backward chaining rule-interpreter can be developed. Using backward chaining we can supply the system with some hypothesis, and the system will attempt to find out if that hypothesis is true. The user will be asked just those questions which are relevant to the hypothesis being considered. Backward chaining is a simple problem-solving strategy, but may be adequate for some tasks.

In a simple backward chaining rule-based expert system there is often a set of possible hypothesized solutions – maybe a set of illnesses that the patient might have. The expert system will consider each hypothesis in turn (e.g., `disease(fred, cold)`), as goals to prove, and try to determine whether or not it might be the case. Sometimes it won't be able to prove or disprove something from the data initially supplied by the user, so it will ask the user some questions (e.g., "have you got a headache?"). The system will normally be told which facts it can reasonably ask the user about – these are sometimes referred to as *askable* facts. Using any initial data plus answers to questions it should eventually be able to conclude which of the possible solutions to the problem is the right one.

The algorithm for this basic system is given below. It would be repeated for each hypothesis G.

To prove G:

- If G is in the current facts it is proved.
- Otherwise, if G is askable then ask the user, record their answer as a new current fact, and succeed or fail according to their response.
- Otherwise, find a rule which can be used to conclude G, and try to prove each of that rule's preconditions.
- Otherwise, fail G.

3.3.1 A Simple Example

This is much better explained through a simple example. Suppose that we have the following rules for diagnosing everyday household emergencies (based loosely on those given in Chapter 2):

R1: *IF coughing THEN ADD smoky*
R2: *IF wet and NOT raining THEN ADD burst_pipe*
R3: *IF NOT coughing AND alarm_rings THEN ADD burglar*
R4: *IF smoky AND hot THEN ADD fire*

We start off with a vague feeling that something is wrong, and that the possibilities are *fire*, *burst_pipe*, and *burglar*. These would be the hypotheses given to the expert system. We'll assume that the system has been provided with no initial facts, so will have to ask the user about the facts about this particular case. We'll further assume that we can directly ask the user whether it is *hot*, whether they are *coughing*, whether it is *wet*, whether it is *raining*, and whether the *alarm rings*.

The simplest backward chaining system would try to prove each hypothesis in turn. First, the system would try to prove *fire*. Rule R4 is potentially useful, so the system would set the new goals of proving *smoky* and *hot*. The first of these, *smoky*, can be concluded using rule R1, so we try in turn to prove *coughing*. This is something we can ask the user:

> Are you coughing?

Suppose the user answers "no". This response would be recorded (in case needed later). The hypothesis *fire* fails, and the system moves on to the next hypothesis: *burst_pipe*. Using rule R2 the user is next asked:

> Are you getting wet?

If the user answers "no" to this too then the hypothesis *burst_pipe* fails, and the system tries *burglar*. Using rule R3 the system sets subgoals *NOT coughing* and *alarm_rings*. The user has already said that they are not coughing, so that information need not be asked again. The system therefore asks:

> Is there an alarm ringing?

If the user answers "yes" the system can conclude that there has been a burglary:

> I conclude that there has been a burglary.

A complete interaction with this tiny system might look like:

> System: Are you coughing?
> User: No.
> System: Are you getting wet?
> User: No.
> System: Is there an alarm ringing?
> User: Yes.
> System: I conclude that there has been a burglary.

In this example there was only one rule that could be used to make a given conclusion. In general (as discussed in Chapter 2) there may be several, and proving a hypothesis involves *searching* through all the possible ways of it could be proved, systematically checking each of them. Search techniques are discussed in more detail in the next chapter. A more realistic system would also have many hundreds of rules, and these rules would contain variables, as discussed in Section 2.4.

3.3.2 Explanation Facilities

Expert systems often have explanation facilities that allow the user to ask *why* it asked some question, and *how* it reached some conclusion. These questions are answered by referring to the system's goals (e.g., to prove *burst_pipe*), the rules being used, and any existing problem data. To illustrate the sorts of facilities commonly provided, we'll elaborate on our simple example above, starting with a simple example dialogue involving *why* and *how* questions and explanations.

> System: Are you coughing?
> User: No.
> System: Are you getting wet?
> User: No.
> System Is there an alarm ringing?
> User: Why?
> System: I'm trying to prove that there has been a burglary. It has been established that it is not the case that you are coughing. Therefore, if there is an alarm ringing then we can conclude that there is a burglary. Is there an alarm ringing?
> User: Yes.
> System: I conclude that there has been a burglary.
> User: How?
> System: This follows from rule R3:
> *IF NOT coughing AND alarm_rings THEN ADD burglar*
> You told me that it is is not the case that you are coughing.
> You told me that there is an alarm ringing.

Providing such an explanation facility involves, at least, recording what rules are used in drawing conclusions, and using these records to compose explanations like the ones above. Giving simple explanations like those above is not very difficult (the answers always have a simple set form), and is sometimes quite useful. However, explanation facilities in expert systems are often not widely used, or are viewed as inadequate by their users. There are a whole number of reasons for this, motivating current research in the area.

One reason is that the explanations just reference the "surface" knowledge encoded in the rules, rather than the "deep" knowledge about the domain which originally motivated the rules (but which is usually not represented). So, the system will say that it concluded X because of rule 23, but will not explain what rule 23 is all about. In the above example, the (slightly odd) rationale behind R3 is that the house may have two kinds of alarm systems, a smoke alarm and a burglar alarm, but that if there's smoke you'll also be coughing! In a system to diagnose diseases the underlying rationale for the rules might be based on a physiological model, while in a system to diagnose faults in a car it might be based on an underlying model of how the car engine works. Unless this knowledge is accessible to the system any explanations will be rather limited.

Another stated reason for the frequent failure of explanation facilities is the fact that, if the user fails to understand or accept the explanation, the system can't re-explain in another way (as people can). Explanation generation is an area of research, concerned with effective communication: how to present things so that people are really satisfied with the expert recommendations and explanations, and how to represent the underlying knowledge required.

3.4 Reasoning Under Uncertainty

In the discussion so far we've assumed that all knowledge is certain. For example, we might say that if it's hot and smoky there is definitely a fire, or that it is definitely hot. However, in many (if not most) practical applications things tend to be vague. If it is hot and smoky it is probably a fire, but it could possibly be a rather unpleasant party. If you are coughing and have a sore throat you probably have a cold, but again you could be at that rather unpleasant party or dingy pub.

Most expert systems therefore require some way of saying that something is probably, but not necessarily, true. Or that some observations (e.g., symptoms) are usually, but not always, associated with some cause (e.g., disease). Some of these techniques will be discussed in the case studies in the next section. However, in this section we'll set the scene by introducing one of the simplest methods, the simple Bayes approach. This method isn't really an AI technique (based directly on well-understood results in probability theory), but can be used to develop simple expert systems. In fact, using this approach you can develop an expert system using a spreadsheet. As the method has often been used for medical expert systems, medical examples will be used throughout.

3.4.1 Background: Basic Probability Theory

The probability of x represents the *degree of belief* in x^2. A probability of 0 means that it can't possibly be true, a probability of 1 means that it is definitely true, and a probability of 0.5 means that it is equally likely to be true as not.

The degree of belief in something will depend on what is already known about the case (i.e., the evidence). If we have a hypothesis H then $P(H)$ gives the degree of belief in H in the absence of any evidence. If we have some evidence E then the probability is represented as $P(H \mid E)$ (the probability of H given E is true). This is referred to as a *conditional* probability. Conditional probability is defined as:

$$P(H \mid E) = \frac{P(H \wedge E)}{P(E)}$$

---

[2]Strictly this is the *subjective* interpretation of probabilities. The *objective* interpretation is more common, and refers to frequencies of events occurring in repeated experiments, but this is not relevant for our purposes.

where $P(H \wedge E)$ is the probability that both H and E are true.

Values for conditional probabilities may be obtained either from experts or from example data. For example, suppose we want to know the probability of a heart attack given that someone reports shooting pain up their arm. We could either ask a doctor for a plausible value, or gather data on hundreds of patients who have reported a shooting pain, and find what proportion were eventually diagnosed as having a heart attack.

In diagnosis problems we very often have available data on the probabilities of various symptoms for different diseases, but may not have the data giving the probabilities of the diseases given the symptoms. (It is easier to obtain suitable data on people who have had heart attacks, than people who have had shooting pains.) Using the above definition for $P(H \mid E)$ we can obtain a formula to find the latter from the former:

$$P(H \mid E) = \frac{P(E \mid H) \times P(H)}{P(E)}$$

This is known as Bayes' theorem.

3.4.2 Independence Assumptions

Normally, of course, there are lots of relevant bits of evidence (e.g., symptoms), which all must be taken into account. We need some way of reasoning with multiple pieces of evidence.

To do this we need to know something about which bits of evidence are *independent* of which others. The notion of independence is very important in probability theory. If two facts E_1 and E_2 are independent of (i.e., have no influence on) each other, then it is very easy to calculate the probabilities of them both being true, i.e., of $E_1 \wedge E_2$:

$$P(E_1 \wedge E_2) = P(E_1) \times P(E_2).$$

So, we only need to know the probabilities of E_1 and of E_2. As an example, the probability of getting two heads in a row when tossing coins is $\frac{1}{2} \times \frac{1}{2} = \frac{1}{4}$. If two facts are not independent (e.g., E_1 = "Carry umbrella", E_2 = "Live in Scotland".) then this simple formula does not apply. We cannot find out $P(E_1 \wedge E_2)$ simply from the probabilities of each separate fact.

For a diagnosis task we are interested in a particular type of independence: the *conditional* independence of a collection of bits of evidence $(E_1 \ldots E_N)$ GIVEN a hypothesis H. If $E_1 \ldots E_N$ are conditionally independent given H, then we have:

$$P(H \mid E_1 \wedge \ldots \wedge E_N) = \frac{P(E_1 \wedge \ldots \wedge E_N \mid H) \times P(H)}{P(E_1) \wedge \ldots \wedge P(E_N)}$$

$$= \frac{P(E_1 \mid H) \times \ldots \times P(E_2 \mid H) \times P(H)}{P(E_1 \wedge \ldots \wedge E_N)}$$

Conditional independence is a convenient simplification, but one that is not always valid. For example, if certain symptoms tend to co-occur then the assumption will be violated. Perhaps if you have a cold then you tend to get either a cough and a sore throat, or neither. If that is the case then they are not conditionally independent, and the above formula will not be accurate.

As it stands we still have to know the *joint* probability of all the evidence (e.g., symptoms) ($P(E_1) \wedge \ldots \wedge P(E_2)$). However, if the possible hypotheses are *exhaustive* and *mutually exclusive* (i.e., everyone has one of the diseases and no-one has more than one) we can simplify the above so that this joint probability is not required. (We find an expression for $P(\neg H \mid E_1 \wedge \ldots \wedge E_N)$ and use this result to eliminate $P(E_1 \wedge \ldots \wedge E_N)$ in the above formula.)

3.4.3   Likelihood Ratios

Bayes' theorem is a little awkward to handle for diagnostic problem solving, so it is commonly reformulated using *likelihood ratios*. We define the *prior* odds of an event H as:

$$O(H) = \frac{P(H)}{1 - P(H)}$$

This is just like the odds given on horses. If the odds on "Speedy" winning are 3:2 then there are three chances of him winning to 2 chances of him not winning. $P(speedywins)$ is the chance that he'll win, and $1 - P(speedywins)$ is the chance that he'll not win. Odds of 3:2 (or 1.5) on a disease mean that three people will have it for every two that don't.

We also need *posterior* odds, which are related to conditional probabilities:

$$O(H \mid E) = \frac{P(H \mid E)}{1 - P(H \mid E)}$$

Maybe the odds of "Speedy" winning given that "Très Vite" has been nobbled are 5:2.

Now, we can consider how adequate some evidence E is for concluding H. The positive *likelihood ratio* (or *level of sufficiency*, LS) is defined to be:

$$LS = \frac{P(E \mid H)}{P(E \mid \neg H)}$$

Using odds and likelihood ratio definitions we can get:

$$O(H \mid E) = LS \times O(H)$$

Given the assumptions of conditional independence we have an equally simple expression for the case where there is more than one bit of evidence. We just multiply together the levels of sufficiency for each bit of evidence, multiply the result by the prior odds, and hey presto, we have the posterior odds for the disease given all the evidence.

Example

Suppose we have obtained the following likelihood ratios (LSs) (from data on $P(E \mid D)$ and $P(E \mid \neg D)$):

	Measles LS	Mumps LS
Spots	15	10
No spots	.3	.5
High Temp.	4	5
No Temp.	.8	.7

We also know that the prior odds of a child having measles are 0.1, and of mumps are 0.05. Now, GIVEN that we know that Fred has spots but no temperature, we can calculate the posterior odds of measles:

$$O(Measles \mid Spots \wedge NoTemp) = 0.1 \times 15 \times .8 = 1.2$$

and of mumps:

$$O(Mumps \mid Spots \wedge NoTemp) = 0.05 \times 10 \times .7 = .35$$

So, there isn't overwhelming evidence for either (as both are associated with having a temperature) but the odds on measles are higher than those on mumps.

Weaknesses of Simple Bayesian Systems

Suppose you used the above formula to develop a simple probabilistic expert system. You could start off with some patient data which would allow you to determine the likelihood ratios and the prior odds of different diseases. If data wasn't available an expert could be asked to make a guess. An expert system could then very simply be developed, perhaps just using a spreadsheet.

However, there are many possible sources of error that might creep into such a system. The symptoms may not in fact be independent given the disease, and the likelihood ratios and prior odds may be inaccurate, based on non-representative or over-small samples of patients or poor guesses of experts. Simple probabilistic methods may give the illusion of precision (giving an output probability of, say, 96.4%), yet these values may still have significant errors. These errors may be critical.

In the simple Bayes formalism, if we don't make assumptions of conditional independence, then we need huge tables of conditional probabilities, giving $P(H \mid E_1 \wedge E_2 \wedge \ldots \wedge E_N)$ for every possible combination of evidence. It just isn't practical to obtain this data. If, say, there were just 16 possible symptoms we'd need a table with $2^{16} = 65,536$ entries for every disease! It is unlikely that an expert would be willing to guess values for all these cases (or could guess them accurately), and it is very unlikely we'd have enough data on past patients to get accurate probabilities for each combination of symptoms.

However, with the simplifying assumptions, simple Bayes systems sometimes work well in narrow and constrained areas, where only a dozen or so diseases are to be considered, with a similar number of relevant symptoms. However, the performance of such systems deteriorates if they are expanded so that more symptoms or more diseases can be considered. This is due to violations in the assumption that the symptoms were independent.

3.5   Three Case Studies in Medicine

So far we've just looked at the basics of a simple kind of rule-based expert system, and introduced some basic ideas about uncertainty. In this section we'll look at the design of three contrasting full-scale practical systems, all used for a medical diagnosis task. This will allow us to look further at how uncertainty can be handled, look at a range of different problem-solving methods, and consider a number of practical issues for expert system development and deployment.

The first system described below, MYCIN, is a pioneering expert system which uses, primarily, a backward chaining rule-based approach, but extends this approach so that uncertainty may be handled. The second, Internist, is another pioneering early system, but one which bases its problem-solving method on human problem solving, and uses a different technique for handling uncertainty. The last, Pathfinder, characterizes a number of more recent systems which use modern statistical techniques for diagnosis, developing on the ideas in the section above. The descriptions of all these systems are necessarily rather simplified, but should illustrate the basic approaches.

3.5.1   MYCIN: A Rule-Based Approach

MYCIN was developed to illustrate how artificial intelligence techniques could be used to solve problems which involve uncertain and incomplete knowledge. It was developed partly in response to the perceived limitations of the simple Bayes systems as described above. It was one of the earliest and most influential expert systems developed, and many expert system shells use methods based on those used in MYCIN.

MYCIN was designed to help physicians in the diagnosis and treatment of patients with certain kinds of bacterial infections. This involves determining the possible organisms involved and choosing the most appropriate drugs. Rapid treatment may be required, so MYCIN was designed to be able to operate on incomplete data, before definitive test results were available. It had to come up with a good "covering" treatment that would deal with all possible infections until an accurate diagnosis could be made.

MYCIN's overall architecture is similar to that in Figure 3.1, and indeed the proposed decomposition of an expert system into these modules was one of the outcomes of the MYCIN project. Pioneering work on knowledge base editors, inference engines and explanation systems was done in the context of this project.

Knowledge Representation
MYCIN's knowledge base consisted of a set of IF–THEN rules, with associated certainty factors. The following is a simplified English version of one of MYCIN's rules:

> IF the infection is primary-bacteremia
> AND the site of the culture is one of the sterile sites
> AND the suspected portal of entry is the gastrointestinal tract
> THEN there is suggestive evidence (0.7) that infection is bacteroid.

MYCIN also included knowledge tables that included basic facts that were needed by the system, such as characteristics of the various bacteria. A special structure called a *context tree* was used to organize case-specific data about the patient.

The above rule includes a numeric value of 0.7 indicating how likely the conclusion is if the conditions are true. Degrees of certainty in MYCIN are represented using *certainty factors*. Facts and rules may have associated certainty factors; a certainty factor of 1 means that something is definitely true, a certainty factor of -1 means that something is definitely not true, while a certainty factor of 0 means that we haven't a clue. Certainty factors are not the same as probabilities, but are related.

If we know the certainty factors of the preconditions (e.g., that the infection is primary-bacteremia), and know the certainty factor of the rule, we can calculate the certainty factor that should be associated with the conclusion.

Suppose we know that the certainty factors associated with the three preconditions are 0.6, 0.5 and 0.8. The first thing we need to do is find the certainty that they are all true. In MYCIN the rule is that we take the *minimum* of the certainty factors of the conjoined preconditions (using AND), so the value associated with the whole precondition is 0.5. The reason for taking the minimum is that our confidence that they are all true should correspond roughly to our confidence in the most weakly held precondition. If we have a rule with a disjunction of preconditions (using OR) we take the *maximum* of the certainty factors. So in general:

$$CF(P_1 \ AND \ \ldots \ AND \ P_N) = MIN(CF(P_1), \ldots, CF(P_N))$$

$$CF(P_1 \ OR \ \ldots \ OR \ P_N) = MAX(CF(P_1), \ldots, CF(P_N))$$

Once we've obtained the certainty factor for the whole precondition we can calculate the certainty of the conclusion, given a particular rule. This is easy – we just multiply the certainty factor of the precondition by the certainty factor of the rule. For the above example we get 0.35. In general, the certainty of a conclusion C given a rule R with precondition P is:

$$CF(C, R) = CF(P) \times CF(R)$$

This is complicated if we have more than one rule which allows us to make the same conclusion. If there are two rules concluding C, which give us certainties (using the above) of $CF(C, R1)$ and $CF(C, R2)$, then, if these are positive, the total certainty factor is:

$$CF(C) = CF(C, R1) + CF(C, R2) - CF(C, R1) \times CF(C, R2)$$

(If one or both of the certainty factors is negative a slightly different formula is used.)

This method for handling uncertainty is regarded as somewhat *ad hoc*. Although it does have roots in probability theory, a lot of assumptions are made about the nature of the data. For some problems this may not be important, as the certainties involved are themselves very uncertain. Experts are unsure how to assign certainty factors to rules, and users are unsure how to assign certainty factors to facts they are asked about. So errors due to a somewhat *ad hoc* calculation may not be as significant as the errors in the original certainties. However, errors in calculations can accumulate, and, while certainty factors may still be useful in simple rule-based systems, current research focuses on developing practical techniques that are based on sounder calculations.

Problem-Solving Strategy
MYCIN uses a fairly simple problem-solving strategy based on backward chaining. Possible bacteria (which might be causing the patient's infection) are considered in turn, and MYCIN tries to prove whether they might be involved using rules such as the one above. So, it might attempt to prove that the organism is *E. coli*, asking the user some questions to determine this, then go on to consider another bacterium, until all are considered. The outcome of this will be a list of possible bacteria and associated certainties.

Once possible diagnoses are determined MYCIN attempts to choose a possible treatment. This consists of two stages: selecting candidate drugs, and then choosing the preferred drugs. At this stage the backward chaining strategy is abandoned in favour of a more data-driven approach. Each organism has an associated list of possible drugs and numbers giving their effectiveness. Given a list of possible organisms these numbers are combined, taking into account all possible organisms and their likelihoods, to determine the best drug or drugs to cover all the possibilities with an adequate degree of certainty.

Example
A (simplified) sample dialogue with MYCIN is given below.

1. M   Patient's name?
2. U: Alan Apt.
...
6. M: Are there any pending cultures for Alan Apt?
7. U: Yes.
8. M: From what site was the specimen for the culture taken?
...
14. M: Please give the date on which the clinical evidence of meningitis first appeared.
15. U: 25 March
16. M: Has the patient had neurosurgery?
17. U: Why?
18. M: This will aid in determining the organisms that might be causing the infection. It has already been established that: the culture is meningitis; organisms were not seen of the pending culture. Therefore if the patient had neurosurgery then there is evidence that the organisms that might be causing the infection are *staphylococcus-coag-pos* (0.75) and *staphylococcus-coag-neg* (0.5). Has the patient had neurosurgery?
19. U: No.
...
26. M: Is the patient a burn patient?
27. U: Yes.
28. M: I have found evidence (rule 507) that treatment should cover for *Diplococcus pneumoniae* causing meningitis. I have found evidence (rule 545) that treatment should cover for *E. coli* causing meningitis.
29. M: Does the patient have focal neurological signs?
30. U: No.
31. M: My preferred therapy recommendation is as follows. In order to cover for *Diplococcus pneumoniae* and *E. coli* give the following in combination: AMPICILLIN Dose 3.85g GENTAMICIN Dose 131mg.

The dialogue is in three stages. The first stage (1-13) elicits basic information about the patient and cultures. This information is used to come up with initial hypotheses (e.g., to only consider meningitis infections). The second stage (14-28) results from backward chaining on these hypotheses, to find the certainty of each. In the last stage (29-31) the system determines and presents appropriate treatments. Alternative therapies will be presented if the first is rejected by the user. At any stage (e.g., 17-18) the user can ask HOW and WHY questions, as discussed in Section 3.3.2.

Evaluation

MYCIN was evaluated by comparing its performance to that of eight members of Stanford's medical school: five faculty members, one research fellow in infectious diseases, one physician and one student. They were given ten randomly selected case histories, and asked to come up with diagnoses and recommendations. These diagnoses, and those produced by MYCIN, were then given to eight independent experts in infectious diseases to evaluate (scoring each diagnosis as acceptable or not). The results showed that MYCIN performed as well as any of the Stanford medical team, and considerably better than the physician or the student.

Despite this positive result, MYCIN has never been used in clinical practice. The reasons are varied, but include:

- A session with MYCIN took half an hour and a great deal of typing! This is unlikely to be acceptable in practice.
- MYCIN's scope was limited and it could not deal with situations that were not explicitly represented in its knowledge base. So it would never, for example, conclude after asking a few questions that it was not a bacterial infection after all, but a nasty cold. In fact MYCIN did not even cover the full spectrum of infectious diseases.
- At that time, MYCIN required more computing power than could be afforded by hospitals.

Follow-on Projects

MYCIN spawned a whole range of follow-on projects, including:

EMYCIN: This was more or less the first expert system *shell*. It provided the basic rule language and interpreter, and allowed MYCIN-like expert systems to be developed much more quickly.

PUFF: A system developed using EMYCIN, to determine the severity of pulmonary disease given data from lung function tests. This system has been used in clinical practice.

GUIDON: This was a tutoring system based on MYCIN. Students would attempt to make diagnoses, MYCIN would be used to check if they were sensible, and Guidon would provide feedback and hints.

NEOMYCIN: This was a rewritten version of MYCIN, which made the underlying problem-solving strategy more explicit.

3.5.2 Internist: Modelling Human Problem Solving

Internist is a large diagnostic program developed at the Pittsburgh School of Medicine. Unlike MYCIN it tries to explicitly capture the way human experts make their diagnoses, using a complex problem-solving strategy based on the technique of *differential diagnosis*. This technique works well when there are a very large number of possible hypotheses (e.g., diseases) to consider. The basic approach is:

- Use available (symptom) data to suggest or *trigger* candidate diseases.
- Determine what other symptoms would be expected given these diseases.
- Gather more data to differentiate between these hypotheses, and update the set of current hypotheses.

Knowledge Representation

Internist represents knowledge about the diseases in question as *disease profiles*, and then uses a complex problem-solving strategy that uses the information in the disease profiles and the evidence found so far.

These disease profiles specify the *findings* (such as symptoms and test results) that are associated with the disease. For each such finding, two numbers are supplied, indicating the correlation between disease and finding. The first number (evoking strength) indicates the likelihood of the disease given that the finding occurs. The second number (frequency) indicates the likelihood of the finding given that the disease occurs. (Convince yourself that these may be different. e.g., a headache only weakly evokes the hypothesis brain tumour, but given a brain tumour a headache is very likely.) Anyway, a numerical value from 0 to 5 is given for both evoking strength and frequency, with an informal interpretation given for each value (for example, an evoking strength of 4 means that "Diagnosis is the overwhelming cause of the given finding"). Evoking strength and frequency are a bit like the conditional probabilities $P(H \mid E)$ and $P(E \mid H)$, but more *ad hoc* techniques are used to manipulate them.

A simplified example disease profile is given below:

Disease profile for ECHINOCOCCAL CYST of LIVER

Finding	Evoking Strength	Frequency
Cough	1	2
Fever	0	2
Jaundice	1	2
Hepatomegaly	1	3

These disease profiles are held in a *disease tree*: a hierarchical classification of disease types. Disease profiles will be supplied both for broad classes of disease (e.g., liver disease) and more specific diseases. The disease knowledge base also contains information about what diseases tend to be associated with what other diseases (so that if one is suggested, the others may be considered), and information about the significance (import) of various findings (so that trivial findings can be disregarded).

Altogether there is knowledge of about 600 diseases and 4500 related findings in Internist. This knowledge base was constructed by a team of physicians, through careful literature review and case discussions. Its construction represents many man-years of effort.

Problem-Solving Strategy

Internist uses this information as follows:

1. The physician enters an initial list of findings, and Internist finds all diseases that are evoked by these findings (i.e., evoking strength > 0).

2. For each such disease hypothesis, Internist creates a *disease model* consisting of four lists:

    (a) Observed findings consistent with the disease.

    (b) Observed findings not associated with the disease.

    (c) Findings associated with the disease which are observed not to be present in patient.

    (d) Findings not yet observed but which are associated with the disease.

3. Based on these lists, each hypothesis is given a score. This score is based on an *ad hoc* scheme which uses the weights of all findings in lists (a)–(c) above, with findings in list (a) contributing positively to the score and the others contributing negatively.

4. The possible hypotheses are sorted, and the *competitors* for the topmost diagnosis are determined. This step acknowledges that the patient may have more than one disease, and it is the diseases which explain the same symptoms as the top disease that should be considered its competitors. Diseases which explain other symptoms may co-exist.

5. Now there will be one or more competing major diagnoses. The strategy now will depend on the number and score of these possible diagnoses. If there is only one, Internist will conclude with that diagnosis. If there is more than one, but the top one is significantly better, Internist will try to confirm the top one, gathering more data about its associated findings. If there are five or more possibilities, Internist will attempt to rule some out. If there are two to four possibilities, Internist will try to discriminate between them, asking questions that will maximize the difference in the resulting scores.

6. When a diagnosis is concluded Internist will remove the patient findings that are explained by the diagnosis from consideration, and start again with any remaining findings (in case the patient has several diseases).

Internist's methods are, on their own admission, *ad hoc*, yet the system is impressive in its performance and in its scope. It covers the whole of internal medicine, and in one study its diagnostic accuracy was shown to be comparable to that of physicians in a major teaching hospital.

QMR

The original Internist system was developed on a large mainframe computer, and was not suitable for use by practitioners. However, in the 1980s the program was adapted to run on PCs as QMR (Quick Medical Reference). Unlike Internist, which was solely a diagnostic tool, QMR can be used in three modes. In its basic mode it can provide diagnostic advice (as Internist). However, it can also be used in other modes, such as as an electronic textbook, listing the symptoms associated with a disease or the diseases associated with a given finding, or just as a tool to explore the relationships between diseases and findings. These modes make use of the detailed medical knowledge base built up during the Internist project, and indeed QMR's authors acknowledge that the most valuable outcome of Internist was its detailed knowledge base. QMR is very much intended to be used as an assistant to the doctor, rather than as an all-knowing expert, and is now used in both clinical practice and education.

3.5.3 Pathfinder: Using Probability Theory

Pathfinder is a system to assist pathologists with the diagnosis of lymph-node related diseases. Given a number of findings (e.g., dead tissue) it would suggest possible diseases (e.g., AIDS). It is interesting because it has explored a range of problem-solving methods and techniques for handling uncertainty.

In the Pathfinder project a variety of techniques were considered for handling uncertainty, including simple Bayes, certainty factors and the scoring scheme used in Internist. These were compared by developing systems based on the different methods, and determining which gave more accurate diagnoses. Surprisingly, simple Bayes did best. A theoretical analysis of the different approaches revealed that they could all be viewed as variants of simple Bayes, and all implicitly incorporated the assumption of conditional independence. In fact, the assumptions made about the data in the non-Bayesian methods were worse than those made in the Bayesian methods. So, for certainty calculations for this kind of problem (dealing with associations between findings and hypotheses), simple Bayes seems best. Yet we know that it has limitations because of the assumptions made about the data.

Simple Bayes, as we have described it, requires that the user indicates, for every possible finding, whether or not that finding is present. Yet this information might be both expensive to obtain (if, for example, a special test had to be done) and tedious to enter. An advantage of Internist was that it would just ask about those findings relevant to the current set of hypotheses and would keep updating this hypothesis set as new data was entered. So questions would only be asked about diseases that seemed likely given data entered so far.

The Pathfinder project both looked at how the dialogue with the user could be controlled so the user is only asked about important findings, and how the basic simple Bayes approach could be developed so that independence assumptions are not required. These two aspects are discussed below.

Controlling the Dialogue

Pathfinder uses a similar basic problem-solving strategy to that used by Internist. It maintains a list of current hypotheses suggested by the findings entered so far, and uses this to suggest further findings which would be useful in differentiating between competing hypotheses. Probabilistic methods are used to score possible hypotheses.

Once the user has entered a few initial findings the system will score all the possible diseases and present the user with an ordered list of the top few hypotheses, along with their probabilities. The user can then either enter further findings (and obtain a new hypothesis list and probabilities) or ask the system which findings would be particularly useful in narrowing the diagnosis. All this is done through a simple menu-based graphical user interface.

To suggest findings that would be useful the system uses a sophisticated technique based on decision theory. The key idea is that entering findings has an associated cost, and the gain from knowing the finding may not outweigh the cost. For example, some findings involve complex tests that either are dangerous to the patient or take too much time. Pathfinder considers the *utility* of the finding, based on how much it contributes to the diagnosis and how important it is to get the diagnosis just right, and the *cost* of the finding. Findings are scored so that the ones recommended to the user are those that bring most benefit for least cost.

In Pathfinder the whole interaction is very much under the control of the user. It is the user who chooses which findings to enter, only asking the system advice if required. This contrasts with Internist, where the dialogue was controlled by the system. In general the mode of interaction used in Pathfinder, with the user in control, is found more acceptable by doctors, emphasizing the role of the expert system as a passive assistant rather than a supplanting expert.

Bayesian Networks

The simple Bayes approach makes assumptions about the data – that evidence is conditionally independent. If these assumptions are not true then this will result in errors. If two findings tend to co-occur given some disease, and both are observed, a simple Bayes system will tend to over-estimate the likelihood of the disease, as it will treat the two findings as independently supporting the hypothesis.

Although the technique was quite successful in Pathfinder, practical methods were sought which would avoid this assumption of independence. A now popular approach is to use a *network* to represent the relationships between the various pieces of evidence and possible hypotheses. These networks, also referred to as *belief networks*, provide an intuitive representation which makes it relatively easy to reason about independence in data, and handle cases where things aren't independent, but are perhaps causally related.

Figure 3.2 illustrates the basic idea. This network is meant to capture the following informally stated medical knowledge: "Metastatic cancer is a possible cause of a brain tumour, and may also tend to result in increased total serum count. In turn, either of these make it more likely that a patient will fall into a coma. Severe headache may also result from a brain tumour."

This network doesn't just include observable symptoms and final diagnoses. It can also include intermediate disease states and measurements (e.g., serum count). If two diseases are causally related (e.g., metastatic cancer and brain tumour) then a link is given between these. The aim is to come up with a moderately simple network that captures information about what states influence what others. Note that there is no link between metastatic cancer and headaches. Although people

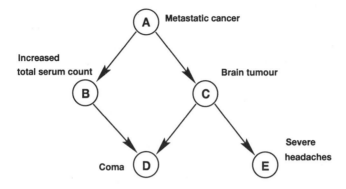

Figure 3.2 *A Simple Bayesian Network.*

with metastatic cancer ARE more likely to get headaches, the claim is that this is only the case because they also tend to have a brain tumour.

Anyway, by specifying the causal relations in this way we are making explicit what facts depend on what, and which are (conditionally) independent. For example, in the figure, E is conditionally independent of A given C. This means that if we know someone has a brain tumour then more evidence for them having metastatic cancer will have no influence on how strongly we believe they will have a headache. Similarly, B is conditionally independent of C given A, so if we know that someone has cancer, then more evidence for them having a brain tumour will not influence our belief in them having an increased serum count.

For each node in a Bayesian network a table of conditional probabilities must be supplied, saying how that node depends on its "parent" nodes. For example, for node D we'd need to supply $P(coma \mid inc.serumcount \wedge braintumour)$, $P(coma \mid inc.serumcount \wedge \neg braintumour)$ and so on. Once these are supplied we can enter findings (e.g., severe headache) and the probabilities of all the other nodes will be updated (e.g., increasing very slightly the probability of brain tumour, and hence the probability of a coma).

As there is no real distinction in this approach between evidence and hypothesis we could also enter the fact that someone has metastatic cancer and find the probability that they have a severe headache. Or enter the fact that they have cancer and a headache and determine the probability that they have a brain tumour.

The network provides us with both an informal and a formal way of reasoning about how some evidence will influence a hypothesis. It is fairly easy to reason informally how belief in one node will influence belief in the others. It is also possible to do accurate calculations to update probabilities in the network. The methods are quite complex, but there are tools available that will allow you to build up a network graphically and have the system take care of the probabilities. It is also feasible to enter all the relevant tables of conditional probabilities (although more are required than for the simple Bayes approach). So Bayesian networks seem to provide a real way forward, overcoming the limitations of simple Bayes systems in a practical manner.

A version of Pathfinder using Bayesian networks proved the most accurate of all the approaches explored, doing significantly better than human expert pathologists.

Pathfinder in Practice

A commercial version of Pathfinder called Intellipath has been developed, and is used fairly widely by practising pathologists – several hundred have been distributed. The system includes both the diagnostic tool and a set of supporting materials such as a library of images, text information about the diseases, references to the literature and a system to produce reports. It is unclear whether it is more the supporting materials or the diagnosis system that has led to the system's relative success.

3.5.4 Summary

In this section we've looked at three contrasting systems for medical diagnosis. Some general conclusions may be drawn concerning problem-solving strategy, reasoning under uncertainty, and practical deployment.

- Although a simple backward chaining system may be successful where there are a relatively small number of hypotheses to consider, where there are many possible hypotheses we need some way of focusing in on those that are currently most likely. Otherwise the system may doggedly pursue an implausible hypothesis, asking irrelevant questions as it goes. Internist provided one approach, based on human problem solving, where questions are asked to differentiate between current hypotheses. Pathfinder uses a complex notion of the utility of information in order to suggest to the user which findings to enter.
- The most theoretically promising approach for handling uncertainty is to use Bayesian networks. However, simpler approaches such as certainty factors may still prove useful for certain problems, particularly where IF–THEN rules provide a natural way to represent expert knowledge.
- Many systems are developed, perform well, but are never used. To be successful in practice a system must integrate with existing systems and working practice, have an easy-to-use interface, require little time to use, and maybe have extra useful features such as textbook information and references to the literature.

The discussion in this section has focused on medical examples. Most of the points apply to all types of expert systems. However, it is important to note that there are lots more problem-solving techniques that have been used for expert systems. We've just considered a few that may be applied to medical diagnosis.

A knowledge engineer should be aware of the whole range of available techniques and tools, and which techniques tend to be suitable for which kinds of task.

3.6 Summary

- Expert systems are used to do tasks normally requiring human expertise, where that expertise is in short supply.
- Suitable problems are ones where the benefits outweigh the costs, cooperative experts are available, users are ready to accept the technology, and the problem itself is highly specialized.
- Expert system development (or knowledge engineering) involves methods for interviewing human experts, selecting suitable problem-solving and knowledge representation methods, rapid prototyping and testing.
- A typical expert system involves the following modules: *knowledge base, inference engine, case-data, explanation system, user interface,* and *knowledge base editor.*
- A simple expert system can be developed using production rules and a backward chaining inference engine. The system will try to prove each of a given set of hypotheses, asking the user questions as it goes.
- For most applications an expert system must be able to represent and reason with uncertain knowledge. A variety of techniques have been developed. The most theoretically advanced is the use of Bayesian networks, which provide an intuitive graphical representation and a sound way of dealing with probabilities.
- Three well-known expert systems in medicine are MYCIN, Internist and Pathfinder. All illustrate very different techniques for problem solving and reasoning with uncertain knowledge. All gave good performance, but getting such systems accepted in practice involves much more than this.

3.7 Further Reading

Most AI textbooks give some discussion of expert systems, although this is often fairly limited. Ginsberg (Ginsberg, 1993) gives a rather brief introduction, but discusses interesting issues concerning the relationship of expert system work to AI in general. Rich & Knight (Rich & Knight, 1991) include a short introduction, including details of knowledge acquisition tools. Luger & Stubblefield (Luger & Stubblefield, 1993) give a fairly extensive introduction to rule-based expert systems, covering similar material to this chapter and give example expert system shells in Lisp and Prolog. Russell & Norvig (Russell & Norvig, 1995) includes a chapter on building a knowledge base, with some interesting discussion on *ontologies* (knowledge-base vocabulary), but the approach is logic-based rather than rule-based.

There are a lot of books devoted to expert systems, but few of them are very good. A thorough and popular book is (Jackson, 1990), which gives both an introduction to knowledge representation in expert systems and a detailed discussion of problem solving, knowledge engineering methods, and various advanced topics. Lucas and van de Gaag (Lucas, & van de Gaag, 1991) give a solid introduction to the knowledge representation methods (with examples in Lisp, Prolog, and psuedo-code), and a good section on reasoning with uncertainty, but limited practical discussion. Turban (Turban, 1992) gives an accessible, although rather lightweight, introduction to applied AI and expert systems in particular, with plenty of discussion of practical AI systems in use, and practical problems in expert system development.

Original articles on the three case studies may be found in (Buchanan & Shortliffe, 1984) (MYCIN), (Miller, 1982) (Internist) and (Heckerman *et al.*, 1992) (Pathfinder). There have been many articles about the lack of progress at getting expert system technology accepted in medicine, including (de Dombal, 1987).

3.8   Exercises

1. A travel agent asks you to design an expert system to help people choose where to go on holiday. Discuss whether this might be a suitable problem for an expert system, and say how you might start acquiring the necessary expert knowledge.

2. Develop a simple set of rules for diagnosing respiratory system diseases given patient symptoms, using the following knowledge of typical symptoms.

   Influenza: Symptoms include a persistent dry cough and a feeling of general malaise.

   Hayfever: symptoms include a runny nose and sneezing. The patient will show a positive reaction to allergens, such as dust or pollen.

   Laryngitis: Symptoms include a fever, a dry cough, and a feeling of general malaise. A "laryngoscopy" will reveal that the person has an inflamed larynx.

   Asthma: Symptoms include breathlessness and wheezing. If it is triggered by an allergen, such as dust or pollen, it is likely to be "extrinsic asthma". "Intrinsic asthma" tends to be triggered by exercise, smoke or a respiratory infection.

Describe how a simple backward chaining interpreter could be used to go through the possible diagnoses, asking the user questions about their symptoms.

If you have an expert system shell available, try implementing a simple diagnosis system based on the above.

3. What do you think are the main problems and limitations of the rule-set developed for question 2? What additional knowledge might be useful to deal with more complex or subtle diagnoses?

4. Compare and contrast the MYCIN and Internist expert systems. Why do you think Internist's strategy is good when there are many hypotheses to consider?

5. What factors do you think should be considered when getting a medical diagnosis expert system accepted in practice? Which of these points would apply to all expert system projects?

6. (Project) Try using a spreadsheet to implement a simple Bayes expert system using the odds-likelihood formulae. Assume that you have data of the likelihood ratios for, say, four diseases given three possible symptoms. (Make up such data if it isn't supplied.) The system should calculate the posterior odds on each disease given the patient's symptoms.

CHAPTER 4

Using Search in Problem Solving

Aims: To introduce both blind and heuristic search techniques, and their use in AI problem solving. Sim-
ple planning and game playing methods will be discussed.

Objectives: You should be able to:

Describe a range of search algorithms, and show how
a search tree would be traversed using these algorithms.

Show how simple puzzles can be formulated as
search problems.

Discuss the limitations of simple search techniques,
and the advantages and disadvantages of the different
methods.

Describe a simple AI planning method, and show
how it can be used to solve simple robot action planning problems.

Explain how minimax search is used in game playing systems, and outline how it may be made more
efficient using Alpha-Beta pruning.

4.1   Introduction

In this section we will switch back to looking at very general techniques that are
important throughout AI. In particular, we will look at how you can use *search*
techniques to try to find a solution to a problem. The general idea here is that
if you know the available actions that you could take to solve your problem, but
don't know which ones will get you to a solution, you can search through all the
possibilities to find one that will give you a solution.

This basic notion of search applies to all sorts of problems. We mentioned in Chapter 2 that backward chaining rule-based systems must have a search strategy so that they can systematically go through the available choices when trying to prove goals. This involves searching for a possible sequence of inference steps which will constitute a proof of some goal. In other applications we may be searching for the sequence of steps that will solve a puzzle, a sequence of moves that will result in winning a game, or a sequence of actions that will allow us to successfully get done the week's shopping. Many of these problems may be expressed in terms of trying to get from some *initial state* (e.g., unsolved puzzle; middle of game; nothing in the fridge) to some *target state* (e.g., solved puzzle; game won; shopping done). We want to search through all the possible actions that could be taken to find a sequence that gets from the initial to target state.

In this chapter we will start off by discussing some basic search techniques and algorithms. Most of these are general-purpose algorithms which may be familiar from other areas of computer science. However, a brief introduction to the relevant background material will be presented. In particular, a basic introduction to *graph theory* terminology will be given, as problems are generally discussed in terms of searching a graph.

To make these more concrete we will discuss these general algorithms by considering how we might search for a good route on a map. We will then show how the methods can be applied to simple problem-solving tasks, and move on to show how more special-purpose algorithms may be used for *planning* and for *game playing*.

4.2 Search Techniques

Suppose we are trying to find our way around a small town with a lot of one-way streets, as illustrated in Figure 4.1. This town has the rather inconvenient feature that, once you've left somewhere, you can never get back there, and that once you're in the park, you can never escape! However, this simplifies our initial discussion of search methods.

Suppose we want to find a possible route from an *initial state* at the library to a *goal state* at the university. (Problem states, for this example, are locations). We can quickly see that the only route involves going via the hospital and the newsagent – but how do we systematically search for such a route, given, perhaps, much more complex maps?

For a simple problem like this, we can *systematically* and *exhaustively* search all possible paths. That is, we can systematically check every state that is reachable from the initial state to find out if it is a goal state. The set of all such states is the *search space*. When the search space is small, relatively simple search techniques are adequate, which try every possible path in a systematic way. These are referred

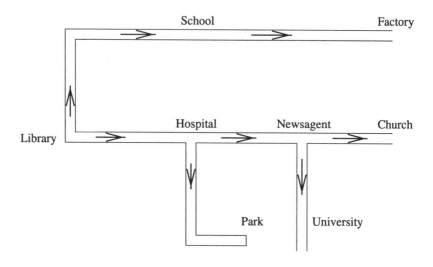

Figure 4.1 *A Simple Search Problem: Finding Routes on a Map.*

to as *brute force* or *blind* search techniques, and include *breadth first* and *depth first* search which are discussed in Section 4.2.2. However, for more complex problems there may be a huge number of possible states to explore – the search space may be very large. It will then not be possible to try them all in a reasonable amount of time. For these problems we may need to use *heuristics* (useful rules-of-thumb) to guess which paths are likely to lead to a solution. Heuristic search algorithms are discussed in Section 4.2.3.

4.2.1   Graphs and Trees

The search algorithms that will be described below are very general, and apply to all sorts of problems. So we need an abstract way of representing search problems so that general-purpose algorithms may be applied, without having to develop a new method for each new problem. *Graphs* are used for this.

There is a lot of terminology used to describe graphs and trees, which is il-lustrated in Figure 4.2. A graph consists of a set of (possibly labeled) *nodes* with *links* between them (these are sometimes referred to as *vertices* and *edges*). The links can be directed (usually indicated by arrows) or undirected. The term *successor* will be used to refer to a neighbouring node, reachable by a link. A *path* is a sequence of nodes connecting two nodes via links (e.g., [a,b,e]). An *acyclic* graph has no *cycles*, i.e., paths linking a node with itself.

A *tree* is a special kind of graph with only one path to each node, usually represented with a special *root node* at the top. Links in a tree are always directed (arrows may be omitted if it is clearly a tree). Relationships between nodes are described using family tree terminology. A is the *parent* of B and F (who are its

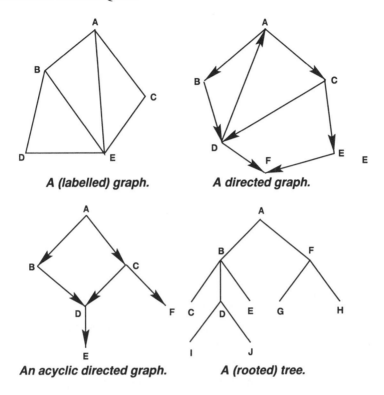

Figure 4.2 *Graphs and Trees.*

children). B is F's *sibling*. A is the *ancestor* of all the other nodes, which are *descendants* of A. Nodes with no children (e.g., C and I) are referred to as *leaf* nodes.

Particularly important terms to note, which will be used throughout this chapter are *node*, *successor*, *path* and *tree*. By using this abstract terminology it is possible to describe very different kinds of problems in the same way, and so use the same algorithm to solve them.

The map in Figure 4.1 can be represented more abstractly as the tree in Figure 4.3 (referred to as the *search tree*). The initial state (*l*) is used as the root node of the tree, which is the *start node* for any search. From this state there are two child nodes *s* and *h*, corresponding to the two directions you can go from the library. From *h* there are two child nodes, as there is a junction at the hospital leading to either the park or the newsagent.

Now, rather than talking about searching for a route from the library to the university, we talk about finding a *path* from a start node *l* (library) to a target node *u* (university). This same graph/tree representation and terminology may be used for many other problems.

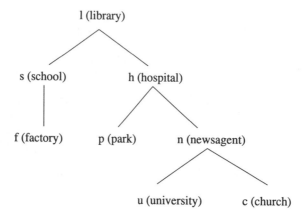

Figure 4.3 *Map Problem Represented as Search Tree.*

4.2.2   Simple Search Techniques: Breadth First and Depth First

The simplest two search techniques are known as *depth first* search and *breadth first* search. They are best introduced by first considering how a *tree* is traversed, then extending this to graphs in general.

The two techniques involve traversing the search tree in different ways, but in both all nodes in the tree will eventually be explored. The algorithms for both methods use a list of nodes that have been found, but have still to be further explored (i.e., their successors haven't been examined yet). This list is sometimes referred to as the *agenda*.

In this section we first examine these two search methods, considering first, basic versions of the algorithms, then two extensions.

Breadth First Search

In breadth first search you would search for a route by trying nodes in following order: l, then s and h, then f, p and n, and finally u and c. (The search might end after node u, which is the goal state.) So, we will first be trying paths of length 1, then 2, then 3 and so on. This is illustrated in Figure 4.4.

The algorithm for breadth first search involves using a *queue* for the agenda. A queue is just a special list where nodes are always added to the end of the list, but removed from the front. Initially the queue contains just the initial state (i.e., $[l]$). Search involves repeatedly taking the first node off the queue, finding that node's successors, and putting them on the end of the queue. This continues until either the first node on the queue is the goal or target state, or the queue is empty. If the first node is the target state the algorithm will signal success (e.g., return TRUE). Otherwise the search fails.

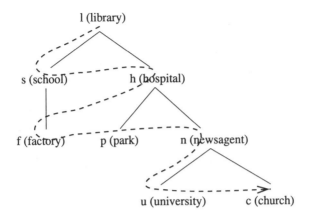

Figure 4.4 *Breadth First Search.*

In our example, initially the queue is:

[l]

We take l off the queue, find that it has successors s and h, and put them on the queue, which is now:

[s, h]

s is taken off the queue, has successor node f, so the new queue is:

[h, f]

h has two successors, p, and n. These are put on the end of the queue:

[f, p, n]

f doesn't have any successors – there was a dead end in the road near the factory – so is just removed from the list. The same happens for p, leaving just n on the queue:

[n]

n has two successors, which are added to the end of the queue:

[u, c]

But u is the goal state, so when that is examined we can exit with success.

The algorithm can be stated more formally as follows:

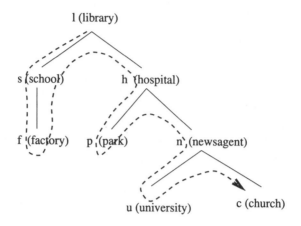

Figure 4.5 *Depth First Search.*

1. Start with *queue* = [initial-state] and *found* = FALSE.
2. While *queue* not empty and not *found* do:

    (a) Remove the first node N from *queue*.

    (b) If N is a goal state then *found* = TRUE.

    (c) Find all the successor nodes of X, and put them on the end of the *queue*.

The algorithm as it stands merely sets a flag *found* to TRUE if it finds a goal state. It may easily be extended to, for example, return the path to the goal state or return all found goal states. The former is considered later in this section. We've also only considered searching trees, and not arbitrary graphs. So we will also see later how it may be extended to handle graphs. However, before looking at these extensions we'll look at depth first search.

Depth First Search
Depth first search is another way of systematically looking for a path from one node to another. In depth first search you keep on going down one path until you get to a dead end. You then back up to try alternatives. (This is referred to as *backtracking*.) Depth first search for our example problem is illustrated in Figure 4.5 – the order of nodes searched is: l, s, f, h, p, n, u, c.

The algorithm for depth first is exactly the same as for breadth first but a *stack* is used rather than a queue, so new nodes are added to the front, rather than the end of the list[1]. Try working through the example problem using depth first search.

Both breadth first and depth first search are simple algorithms that will eventually find a path if there is one (and if the search tree is finite). However, sometimes

---

[1] Alternatively, a simple recursive algorithm can be used. However, we will stick with an explicit stack, so that comparisons between the algorithms are clearer.

one of the two may be more appropriate than the other. The choice of algorithm depends on a number of factors:

- Are you looking for the shortest path? If so, breadth first may be better as it will find the shortest path first.
- Is memory likely to be a problem? Depth first search generally requires much less memory.
- Do you want to find a solution quickly? If so, the choice of algorithm gets complex! Depth first may be faster if there are many paths that lead to solution states, but all are quite long. Breadth first may be faster if there is one short path to the target, but within a large and deep search space.

There are many variants of breadth and depth first search that may be useful in certain situations. For example, you can set a *depth limit* in depth first search so it backs up when it gets to nodes further than the specified distance from the initial state. A variant of this is an algorithm called *iterative deepening* which repeats depth first search with gradually increasing depth limits. In spite of the apparent waste in repeating bits of search this is a very useful algorithm, as it both requires little memory (like depth first) and finds the shortest path first (like breadth first).

Returning the Path

As mentioned above, the algorithm so far, whether depth or breadth first, just indicates whether or not there is a path. In general we may want it to return the successful path that allows us to get from the initial to goal state. There are a number of ways to do this – look in any text on algorithms. We'll just mention one that is particularly straightforward in a Prolog implementation of the search algorithm. What we can do is make an item in the agenda be a path rather than a state – we can still check for success by, for example, checking whether the last element of the path is the goal state, and we can modify our search algorithms to return the path once a successful one is found. We'd start with an agenda[2] like:

$$[[l]]$$

(i.e., one item in the agenda, which is a path with one item in it). Then after finding l's successors we'd have:

$$[[l, s], [l, h]]$$

and so on. At each stage we'd check whether the last item in the first path is the goal state.

Searching Graphs

So far we've assumed that we are searching a *tree*, and not an arbitrary graph. In a tree, we can't get to the same node by two different routes, and we can't go in circles and get back from a node we started from.

---

[2]From now on the more general term agenda will be used – a stack or queue might be used for this.

However, most problems involve searching general graphs. Consider our simple map search problem. Clearly most maps allow us both to get to the same place by more than one route, and to get back to where we came from by taking a circular route. Most AI problems (where we're searching for a sequence of actions to achieve some state) also involve graph search rather than simple tree search.

If we use our simple tree search algorithms when searching arbitrary graphs then at best they will be less efficient (we will redo work already done) and at worst we'll get caught in infinite loops. To address the infinite loop problem, we can make a very small modification to our algorithm: we avoid adding a node to a path if it already appears on the path. (This is straightforward if your agenda consists of paths rather than just nodes.)

However, this doesn't address the efficiency problem. Consider the graph in Figure 4.6 (which corresponds to a map with one-way streets, but more than one route to the hospital). If we use a simple depth first search method we might first search nodes l, s, h, n and c, back up and search node f, but then try nodes h, n and c again, repeating part of the search. (Try working through what happens for this example, given the simple depth first search algorithm.)

The problem is that we have no record of the fact that h, n, and c have already been searched. To get round this problem we just keep such a record. For example, we could maintain a list of nodes already explored – this will be referred to as the *visited* list (the term *closed* list is also sometimes used). The algorithm can now be modified so that nodes that are already on the visited list are not explored further. A basic version of this revised algorithm, this time for depth first search, is given

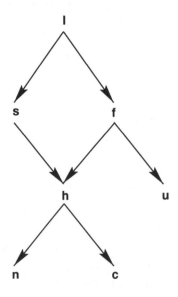

Figure 4.6 *Example Search Graph*

below. It may of course be extended to return the path, as outlined above.

1. Start with *agenda* = [initial-state] and *found* = FALSE.
2. While *agenda* not empty and not *found* do:
   (a) Remove the first node N from *agenda*.
   (b) If N is not in *visited* then:
      i. Add N to *visited*.
      ii. If N is a goal state then *found* = TRUE.
      iii. Put N's successors on the front of the *stack*.

Summary

To summarize so far, search techniques are used in AI to find a sequence of steps that will get us from some initial state to some goal state(s). You can use various search algorithms to do the search. We've so far discussed simple breadth first search and depth first search. These are both systematic, exhaustive search techniques that will eventually try all the nodes in the search space (if it's finite). The appropriate algorithm will depend on the problem you are trying to solve, such as whether you want the shortest path.

4.2.3 Heuristic Search

So far we have looked at two search algorithms that can in principle be used to systematically search the whole search space. Sometimes, however, it is not feasible to search the whole search space, as it is too big – imagine searching every possible road and alley in a 400-mile circumference around London when looking for a route to a house in Edinburgh. Where the search space is too big to search every node it may be possible to construct some scoring function that can be used to provide an estimate as to which paths or nodes seem promising. Then the promising nodes are explored before the less promising ones. Search methods that use such a scoring function are referred to as *heuristic search* techniques .

The basic idea of heuristic search is that, rather than trying all possible search paths, you try to focus on paths that seem to be getting you nearer your goal state. You generally can't be sure that you are really near your goal state – it could be that you'll have to take some highly complicated and circuitous sequence of steps to get there. But we might be able to have a good guess. Heuristics are used to help us make that guess.

To use heuristic search you need an *evaluation function* that scores a node in the search tree according to how close to the target/goal state it seems to be. This will just be a guess, but it should still be useful. For example, for finding a route between two towns a possible evaluation function might be an "as the crow flies" distance between the town being considered and the target town. Then, routes that seem to get you nearer the target are explored before those that get you further from the target. This strategy may not always work – maybe there aren't any good roads from this town to your target town, and you have to first go away from your destination in order to get onto the right road. However, it provides a quick way of guessing that helps in the search, and will tend to result in a solution being found faster.

There are a large number of different heuristic search algorithms, of which we'll go through three: hill climbing, best first search and A*. We'll assume that we are searching trees rather than graphs (i.e., there aren't any loops etc.). However, the algorithms can be simply extended for graph search by using the methods outlined in Section 4.2.2.

Hill Climbing

In hill climbing, the basic idea is to always head towards the best successor node (and only if that node is better than the current one). So, looking at Figure 4.1, if you are at the hospital trying to get to the church, and you could either move along the road to the newsagent or along the road to the park, then you should move to the newsagent, as it is nearer to the church than either the hospital or the park. The basic algorithm is as follows:

1. Start with *current-state* = initial-state.
2. Until *current-state* = goal-state OR there is no change in *current-state* do:

   (a) Get the successors of *current-state* and use the evaluation function to assign a score to each successor.

   (b) If one of the successors has a better score than *current-state* then set the new *current-state* to be the successor with the best score.

Note that the algorithm does not attempt to exhaustively try every node and path, so no list of nodes to explore is maintained – just the current state. If there are loops in the search space then using hill climbing you shouldn't encounter them – you can't keep going up and still get back to where you were before.

Hill climbing terminates when there are no successors of the current state which are better than the current state itself. This is often a problem. For example, suppose we were looking for a route from the library to the university, using "as the crow flies distance to target" as the evaluation function. Initially the current state would be library, then hospital, and then park (as this brings us nearer to the park than the newsagent would). But this is a dead end, and there is nowhere to try now that would bring us nearer to the university. So the algorithm would halt without success. This would also happen for the map in Figure 4.7, if we were trying to get from the library to the park. In this case we'd move from the library to the school, but then halt, as there is no other location nearer to the park.

These problems are essentially the result of *local maxima* in the search space – points which are better than any surrounding state, but which aren't the solution. There are some ways we can get round this (to some extent) by tweaking or extending the algorithm a bit. We could use a limited amount of backtracking, so that

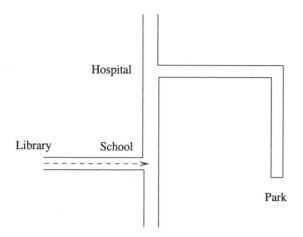

Figure 4.7 *Map Illustrating Limitations of Hill Climbing.*

we record alternative reasonable looking paths which weren't taken and go back to them. Or we could weaken the restriction that the next state has to be better by looking ahead a bit in the search – maybe the next but one state should be better than the current one. None of these solutions is perfect, and in general hill climbing is only good for a limited class of problems where we have an evaluation function that fairly accurately predicts the actual distance to a solution.

Best First Search

Best first search is a little like hill climbing, in that it uses an evaluation function and always chooses the next node to be that with the best score. However, it is exhaustive, in that it should eventually try all possible paths. It uses a list of nodes that are still to be further explored (as in depth/breadth first search), but rather than always adding new nodes on the front or rear, and removing nodes from the front, it always removes the *best* node from the list, i.e., the one with the best score. For those familiar with data structures, the algorithm makes use of a *priority queue*, rather than a stack or a simple queue – however, we'll use the more general term *agenda*. The successors of the best node will be evaluated (i.e., have a score assigned to them) and added to the agenda.

The basic algorithm is as follows:

1. Start with *agenda* = [initial-state].
2. While *agenda* not empty do:

   (a) Remove the best node from the *agenda*.

   (b) If it is the goal node then return with success. Otherwise find its successors.

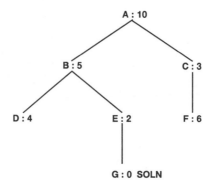

Figure 4.8 *Search Tree Illustrating Best First Search.*

(c) Assign the successor nodes a score using the evaluation function and
add the scored nodes to *agenda.*

Suppose we have the search tree in Figure 4.8. Here links between nodes
illustrate possible successor states. A node label such as B:5 means that the node
name is B and it has an estimated cost to solution of 5 (so a lower value is better).

Suppose our goal state is G. If we searched this search space using breadth
first search then the nodes would be searched in the following order: A, B, C, D,
E, F, G. Using depth first search the order would be: A, B, D, E, G. For both of
these the scores on nodes are ignored. Using simple hill climbing a solution would
never be found – there is a local maximum at C where it would get stuck. Using
best first search the order would be: A, C, B, E, G. You should verify this using the
algorithm above.

If you have a good evaluation function, best first search may drastically cut
down the amount of search that you have to do to find a solution. You may not find
the best solution (or at least, the first solution found may not be the best), but if a
solution exists you will eventually find it, and there is a good chance of finding it
quickly. Of course, if your evaluation function is no good then you are just as well
off using simpler search techniques such as depth first or breadth first. And if your
evaluation function is very expensive (i.e., it takes a long time to work out a score)
the benefits of cutting down on the amount of search may be outweighed by the
costs of assigning a score.

The A* Algorithm
In its simplest form as described above, best first search is useful, but doesn't take
into account the distance of the path so far when choosing which node to search
from next. So, you may find a solution but it may be not a very good solution.
There is a variant of best first search known as A* which attempts to find a solution
which minimizes the total cost of the solution path. ("Cost" is intended as a general
notion – for map problems this might be the distance.)

In the A* algorithm the evaluation function consists of two parts. The first part is based on the cost associated with getting from the start node (corresponding to the initial state) to the node in question. The second part is an *estimate* of the cost from this node to the target node. The total score is a (possibly weighted) sum of these two parts, giving an estimate of the total cost from start to target going via the node in question. So, if $g(Node)$ gives the cost from start node to Node, and $h(Node)$ gives the estimated cost from Node to target, the total score $f(Node)$ is:

$$f(Node) = g(Node) + h(Node)$$

The A* algorithm is essentially the same as the simple best first algorithm, but we use this slightly more complex evaluation function. (Our best node will be the one with the *lowest* cost/score.) To illustrate what A* gains us, consider the search tree in Figure 4.9 where successor links are labelled with the cost of getting between nodes and the scores attached to nodes are again an estimate of the cost to solution.

If we use simple best first search we would search the nodes in the following order: A, B, D, E, F. As F is our goal state we'd have a solution, but it would not be a particularly good one. It will have a path cost of 13 (2+4+3+4). If we use A*, then the nodes will be searched in the following order: A, B, C, G, F', with the solution path found being the that with lowest cost (7). In fact, the A* algorithm guarantees to find the shortest path first. However, to make this true we have to ensure that $h(Node)$ does not *overestimate* the cost to the solution. The definition of the A* algorithm includes this requirement.

A* may be compared with both breadth first and best first search. In breadth first search, if the cost of traversing each link is the same, the lowest cost solution will be found first. However, it may not be found very quickly. In best first search

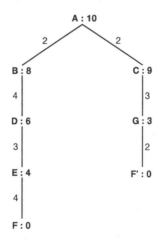

Figure 4.9 *Search Tree Illustrating A* Search.*

some solution should be found quickly, but it may not be a very good solution. In A* we should find a good solution and find it quickly.

4.3 Problem Solving as Search

So far we have described several search algorithms, but not how they are used in solving problems. In general, search techniques are used to find a sequence of actions that will get us from some initial state to some goal state. The actions may be physical actions (such as move from town A to town B, or put block C on the table) or may be more abstract actions, like theorem-proving steps (we may be searching for a sequence of steps that will allow us to prove X from the set of facts S).

There are many different ways search techniques that can be used in problem solving. This section will start by looking at how simple search techniques may be used to solve puzzles, using a very simple representation of the possible actions that are allowed. Then we'll show how the approach may be extended for slightly more complex *planning* problems, changing the search algorithm and the way actions are represented. Finally we'll look at game playing systems – where there is an opponent out to foil any plan.

In all the methods discussed a node in the search space will be some formal description of the current state of the problem. For a board game playing system this might be a description of the current state of the board; for a puzzle it might be a description of the current state of the objects in the puzzle. Successor nodes will be possible new states, which can be reached from the current state by taking some action (e.g., making a move in a game). The search space is sometimes referred to as the *state space* as it captures all the possible states or situations you could get into, and the methods referred to as *state space* search techniques.

4.3.1   State Space Search Techniques

Simple state space search techniques (where nodes in the search space represent the problem state) are often illustrated by showing how they can be used in solving puzzles of the sort you find in intelligence tests. One such puzzle is the water jug problem:

> "You are given two jugs, a 4-gallon one and a 3-gallon one. Neither has any measuring markers on it. There is a tap that can be used to fill the jugs with water. How can you get exactly 2 gallons of water into the 4-gallon jug".

Given such a problem, we have to decide how to represent the problem state (e.g., amount of water in each jug), what the initial and final states are in this

1.	Fill the 4-gallon jug.	$\{X, Y\} \rightarrow \{4, Y\}$
2.	Fill the 3-gallon jug	$\{X, Y\} \rightarrow \{X, 3\}$
3.	Empty the 4 gallon jug into the 3-gallon jug.	$\{X, Y\} \rightarrow \{0, X+Y\}$ (if $X+Y \leq 3$)
4.	Empty the 3-gallon jug into the 4-gallon jug.	$\{X, Y\} \rightarrow \{X+Y, 0\}$ (if $X+Y \leq 4$)
5.	Fill the 4-gallon jug from the 3-gallon jug.	$\{X, Y\} \rightarrow \{4, X+Y-4\}$ (if $X+Y > 4$)
6.	Fill the 3-gallon jug from the 4-gallon jug.	$\{X, Y\} \rightarrow \{X+Y-3, 3\}$ (if $X+Y > 3$)
7.	Empty the 3-gallon jug.	$\{X, Y\} \rightarrow \{X, 0\}$
8.	Empty the 4-gallon jug.	$\{X, Y\} \rightarrow \{0, Y\}$

Figure 4.10 *Actions for Water Jug Problem.*

representation, and how to represent the actions available in the problem. Actions are represented by specifying how they change the problem state.

This particular puzzle is based on a simple problem-solving domain where the problem state can be represented simply as a pair of numbers giving the amount of water in each jug (e.g., $\{4, 3\}$ means that there is 4 gallons in the 4-gallon jug and 3 in the 3-gallon jug). The initial state is $\{0,0\}$ and the final state is $\{2,X\}$ where X can take any value. There are only a small number of available actions (e.g., fill the 4-gallon jug), and these can be simple represented as 8 *rules* or *operators* which show how the problem state changes given the different actions. These are listed in Figure 4.10.

Rules such as $\{X, Y\} \rightarrow \{X, 0\}$ mean that we can get from a state where there are X gallons in the first jug and Y in the second jug to a state where there are X gallons in the first and none in the second, using the given action. If there is a condition such as (if $X+Y \leq 3$) this means that we can only apply the rule if that condition holds. We only consider actions that cause a change in the current state.

Note that in puzzles such as this we restrict our set of actions to ones that might actually be useful in solving the problem. It won't help just pouring a random amount of water onto the ground, as then we won't know where we are! The programmer has to supply most of the intelligence, in the way the problem is represented and the algorithm chosen to solve it.

Now, how do we use our standard search techniques discussed earlier? The notion of a "successor state" is a little more obscure here than in the map domain. We have to look at all our actions, and find ones that apply given the current state. We can then use the rules above to find the states resulting from those actions. A particular node in the search tree, rather than being just the name of a town, will now be the representation of a particular state (e.g., $\{2, 3\}$) (see Figure 4.11).

This should all be clear when we try to solve the problem. We'll use depth first search first, and make the items on the agenda be *paths* from the initial state to the current state, rather than just the current state, and check for loops within each

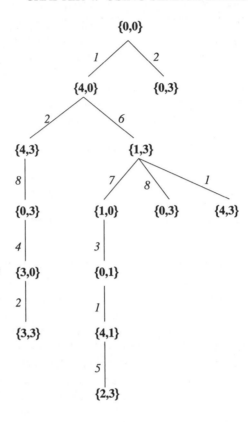

Figure 4.11 *Search Tree for Jugs Problem.*

path. Other search techniques (as discussed in Section 4.2) could also be used.

Initially the jugs are both empty, so the initial state is $\{0, 0\}$, and the agenda is:

agenda = [[$\{0, 0\}$]]

(All the brackets are because a *state* is represented as $\{0,0\}$, a *path* with just that one state in it is [$\{0,0\}$], and an agenda or list of such paths is [[$\{0,0\}$]].)

Anyway, our goal state is $\{2, X\}$, where X can take any value. To start problem solving, we remove the first path from *agenda* and look for possible *extensions* to that path. A possible extended path is one that is the same as the old one, but has an extra node at the end of it, such that that node is a *successor* of the last node in the old path. There may be several such possible extended paths.

There are two actions that you can take from $\{0,0\}$ that will change the state of the world – filling the 3-gallon or filling the 4-gallon jug. Possible successors are $\{4, 0\}$ and $\{0, 3\}$, so the new agenda is:

agenda = [[$\{0,0\}$,$\{4,0\}$], [$\{0,0\}$,$\{0,3\}$]]

From {4, 0} actions 2, 6 and 8 apply. Possible next states are: {4, 3}, {1, 3}, {0, 0}. {0, 0} is already on the path (so there would be a loop), so that one is thrown away, and the new agenda is:

agenda = [[{0,0},{4, 0},{4,3}], [{0,0},{4,0},{1,3}],[{0, 0},{0,3}]]

Now, from {4, 3} we can apply actions 7 and 8. Action 7 will get us back to {4, 0} which already on the path, so that one is ignored. Action 8 will get us to {0,3}, so in the new agenda the first item is replaced with [{0,0},{4,0},{4,3},{0,3}]. From {0,3} we can get to {3,0} or {4,3} or {0,0}. Only {3,0} is a new state, so the new agenda is now:

agenda = [[{0,0},{4,0},{4,3},{0,3},{3,0}],
        [{0,0},{4,0},{1,3}],[{0,0},{0,3}]]

Now, from {3,0} we can get to {0,3}, {0,0} and {3,3} (pour jug 1 into jug 2; empty jug 1; fill jug 2). Only {3,3} is a new state, so the agenda becomes:

agenda = [[{0,0},{4,0},{4,3},{0,3},{3, 0},{3,3}],
        [{0,0},{4,0},{1,3}],[{0,0},{0,3}]]

From {3,3} we're stuck. All of the reachable states are already on the path. So we remove that whole path from the agenda and look at the next path. From {1,3} we can reach {1,0}, {0,3}, {4,3}, all of which are new states on the path. So there are three possible extended paths and the agenda is:

agenda = [[{0,0},{4,0},{1,3},{1,0}], [{0,0},{4,0},{1,3},{0,3}],
        [{0,0},{4,0},{1,3},{4,3}],[{0,0},{0,3}]]

From {1,0} we can reach a new state {0,1} (pour jug 1 into jug 2), and from there a new state {4,1} (fill jug 1). And from there we can fill jug 2 from jug 1, leaving 2 gallons in jug 1, and we get to {2,3}! This is the solution we were looking for. We have 2 gallons in the 4-gallon jug. The portion of the search tree explored is given in Figure 4.11. The numbers in italics indicate the relevant actions.

So we have found one solution to the problem – fill the 4-gallon jug, fill the 3-gallon from the 4-gallon, empty the 3-gallon, empty the 4-gallon into the 3-gallon, fill the 4-gallon and fill the 3-gallon from the 4-gallon again. In fact, because we carefully formulated the problem, and ruled out actions that resulted in old states or no change, there wasn't too much search involved. Problems which do involve a lot of search would just be too tedious to go through! Hopefully however the example will have given an idea of how simple problems are approached using search techniques. You have to decide on a representation of the problem state, of the available actions for that problem, and systematically go through all possible sequences of actions to find one that will get from the initial to target state.

Note that in the solution to this problem we sometimes re-examined states that had already been explored. For example, the state $\{0,3\}$ is on the explored tree on three branches. A lot of work is done that has been done before (e.g., checking if there is a solution starting from the state $\{0,3\}$.). We could have avoided this by using a *visited* list, as outlined in Section 4.2.

In the water jug problem there is no real need to use a heuristic search technique – the domain is sufficiently constrained that you can go through all possibilities pretty quickly. In fact, it's hard to think what a good evaluation function would be. If you want 2 gallons in the jug, does it mean you are close to a solution if you have 1 or 3 gallons? Many problems have the property that you seem to have to undo some of the apparent progress you have made if you are to eventually get to the solution (e.g., empty out the jug when you've got 1 gallon in it). Heuristic search is often useful in problem solving, but it may be better to try to carefully formulate the problem, so that the search space is small and simple search techniques can be applied.

There are lots of other problems that have been solved using similar techniques, and which are discussed in many longer AI textbooks. One is given in the exercises at the end of the chapter.

Complexity Problems

The techniques that we have described can be applied to many problem-solving tasks. However, for realistic tasks we often run into difficulties. One problem relates to the complexity of the algorithms. For *brute force* search techniques such as breadth first and depth first we may end up having to search an enormous number of nodes in the search space to find a solution. For example, if there are (on average) n successors to every node in the search space, and our solution is at depth d, then in breadth first search we may need to search n^d nodes. If n is, say, 20 and d is 6 then we may need to search over 60 million nodes. For depth first search we may be luckier, and happen to hit on a solution sooner, but then if there isn't a solution on the first branch we try we may end up having to search even more nodes. Graph search techniques, where we avoid re-examining already searched nodes, may help for some problems, but carry some overhead in maintaining and checking a list of nodes already encountered. Heuristic search methods may be useful, but only when the evaluation functions are good.

The average number of successor states for nodes in the search space is known as the *branching factor*. For search to be tractable we want our search space to have a fairly small branching factor. The branching factor will depend on how a problem is formulated. In state space search the branching factor can be reduced by applying some (human!) intelligence when specifying the rules or operators for deriving successor states – we want to make sure any pointless actions/successor states are not even considered in the search. It may also be reduced by choosing appropriately whether to search forward, from the initial state, or backwards, from the goal state (either is often allowable). The branching factor in each case may be very different.

If none of this helps then we have a *combinatorial explosion*! We just have too many combinations to try, and the deeper in the tree we search the worse it gets. Largely because of this problem, general-purpose search techniques are often inadequate for serious problem solving. They need to at least be augmented with more specialized, domain-specific problem-solving techniques.

4.3.2 Planning Techniques

Planning, in AI, is the problem of finding a sequence of primitive actions to achieve some goal. This sequence of actions will be the system's plan, which can then be executed. Planning is often discussed in the context of robotics, where it is a physical robot which will execute the plan. However, it is important in many areas of AI – for example, in natural language understanding it is important to reason about peoples' plans and goals in order to best make sense of what they say.

State-space search may be viewed as a simple planning technique. However, generally in the AI literature the term "planning" is reserved for slightly more sophisticated stuff, where actions in particular are represented in a more complex way. To introduce AI planning mechanisms we'll describe a simple planning method based on the *means–ends analysis* (MEA) approach to problem solving, and a representation of actions introduced in one of the first AI planning systems called STRIPS.

Means–ends analysis is an approach to problem solving which, rather than blindly searching through all possible actions, focuses on actions that reduce the *difference* between the current state and the target state. Another feature is that if an action is found that reduces this difference, then it will be considered even if it can't be applied in the current state. Getting to a state where the useful action can be applied is set as a new subproblem to solve.

Means–ends analysis can be applied to a whole range of problem-solving tasks – indeed, it was designed as part of a general model of how people solve problems (the GPS or General Problem Solver). However, we will just describe a variant which uses the STRIPS representation of actions, and is applied to simple robot planning tasks. A typical task might involve stacking a number of blocks, or moving some objects between rooms.

The technique uses the basic ideas of state-space search. It is concerned with searching for a path from some initial state to some desired final or target state, checking through the different possible actions that could be taken to see which sequence of actions leads to the right result. *Means–ends analysis* is the technique used to control the search.

In simple planning systems the problem state can be represented as a list of facts that are true, e.g.:

> [at(robot, living_room), at(beer, kitchen), at(fred, living_room), door_closed(kitchen, living_room)]

This might represent a state where Fred is in the living room with his robot, but the beer is in the kitchen and the door to the kitchen is shut.

Given this new representation of the problem state (as a list of true facts) we need a slightly more sophisticated way to represent actions. Actions are now represented by operators that give the *preconditions* of the action and the *effects* of that action on the problem state. An effect may be to *add* a new fact to the problem state, or to *delete* a fact. So, if we assume that the only actions allowed in our example are "robot opens/closes door", "robot moves from one room to another" and "robot carries object from one room to another" then we can have the following operators to describe the possible actions:

Operator	Preconditions	Add	Delete
open(R1, R2)	at(robot, R1) door_closed(R1, R2)	door_open(R1, R2)	door_closed(R1, R2)
close(R1, R2)	at(robot, R1) door_closed(R1, R2)	door_closed(R1, R2)	door_open(R1, R2)
move(R1, R2)	at(robot, R1) door_open(R1, R2)	at(robot, R2)	at(robot, R1)
carry(R1, R2, O)	door_open(R1, R2) at(robot, R1) at(O, R1)	at(robot, R2) at(O, R2)	at(robot, R1) at(O, R1)

Suppose our target state involves Fred with his beer in the living room, his robot by his side, the door closed.

[at(beer, living_room), at(fred, living_room), at(robot, living_room), door_closed(kitchen, living_room)]

Means–ends analysis tries to find an operator whose effects reduce the difference between the current and target states. At the moment, the beer is in the wrong place! The only operator that can shift the beer is the "carry" operator. If it could be applied, then we'd in fact arrive at our goal state. Unfortunately the robot is in the wrong room, and the door is shut.

However, the fact that we can't apply an operator now doesn't stop us. We set the unsatisfied *preconditions* of the actions as new goals to solve. So we recursively try to call the means–ends algorithm with the preconditions of the action as the target state. That is, we try to solve:

Initial state:

[at(robot, living_room), at(beer, kitchen), at(fred, living_room), door_closed(kitchen, living_room)]

Target state:

[open_door(kitchen, living_room), at(robot, kitchen)]

We now try to find a sequence of actions that will make this new target state true. Without going through the details, if we choose open(kitchen, living_room) and move(living_room, kitchen) then the (intermediate) target state is true.

Now we have to finish the plan. We find what state we get if we apply the operators worked out so far to our initial state. In our example this gives us:

[at(robot, living_room), at(beer, living_room), at(fred, living_room),
door_open(kitchen, living_room)]

We're almost at our target state, but the door is now open. We therefore have to complete the plan by finding a way to close the door. Eventually we will have a completed plan:

open(kitchen, living_room)

move(living_room, kitchen)

carry(kitchen, living_room, beer)

close(kitchen living_room)

This involved first finding an action in the *middle* of the plan: carry(kitchen, living_room, beer). Then the start and end parts of the plan are completed.

This can be illustrated as follows:

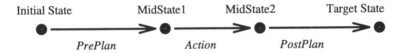

The overall algorithm used is the following:

To find_plan(Initial_State, TargetState)

- If all the goals in TargetState are true in InitialState then succeed.
- Otherwise:

  1. Select an unsolved Goal from TargetState.

  2. Find an Action that adds Goal to the current state.

  3. Enable Action by finding a plan (PrePlan) that achieves its preconditions, i.e., find_plan(InitialState, Preconditions). Let MidState1 be the result of applying that plan to InitialState.

  4. Apply Action to Midstate1 to give MidState2.

  5. Find a plan (PostPlan) from MidState2 to TargetState.

  6. Return a plan consisting of PrePlan, Action and PostPlan.

Many subsequent AI Planning systems have been based on a modified version of this algorithm. Extensions to the basic algorithm include:

Planning with goal protection: where the algorithm includes a check that an action being considered doesn't accidentally undo a goal that was achieved earlier.

Nonlinear planning: where the algorithm does not commit to the order that actions occur in the plan unless one action has to precede another to enable the other's preconditions.

Hierarchical planning: where the plan is developed in outline first, and then the details are filled in.

Reactive planning: where the plan can be modified if the state of the world unexpectedly changes or failures occur.

In many modern planners a node in the search space no longer represents the current problem state, but may represent a possible partially completed plan. Planning involves searching through possible ways that a partial plan may be developed. This has proved a more flexible framework for practical planning, and is discussed in many of the references at the end of the chapter (e.g., (Russell & Norvig, 1995) (ch.11)).

Practical Planning

When planning systems are applied to practical real-life problems the simple search methods discussed in this section prove inadequate to the task, and more complex methods must be used. An example practical planning system is O-Plan, developed at Edinburgh. In O-Plan (and its predecessor, Nonlin), the objective is to gradually develop and refine a partially completed plan. This plan may initially be very sketchy, with details missing, and no fixed order given for the actions. It can then be developed or repaired in various ways. For example, an action in the plan may be *expanded* to give more detail about how it should be carried out.

O-Plan has been used for a variety of applications, for example constructing plans for disaster recovery planning. In this application the system first selects a basic *template* outlining a basic plan for the particular type of disaster (e.g., gas explosion). This template is then filled in, expanded and refined.

4.3.3 Game Playing Systems

As a final example of how search techniques can be used in problem solving we'll consider game playing systems. The basic approach applies to two-person adversarial games where both players know the state of the game. Many board games such as chess, draughts, and Go fit into this category (two players are competing, and both can see the board).

Games are rather different from the problems that have been looked at so far in this chapter, as there is an opponent involved who will try to foil any plan! So, although it is possible to work out a sequence of actions to achieve a winning state, it is highly likely that a move of your opponent will prevent you from carrying out that plan. Some method is needed for selecting good moves that stand a good chance of achieving a winning state whatever the opponent does.

Game playing problems can still be categorized in terms of search trees. Figure 4.12 gives part of a simple search tree (or *game tree*) for a game of noughts and crosses. Note how the levels in the tree alternate between the two players.

Figure 4.13 illustrates the complete game tree for a hypothetical very simple game where a win is possible in just two moves. (The possible game states are just

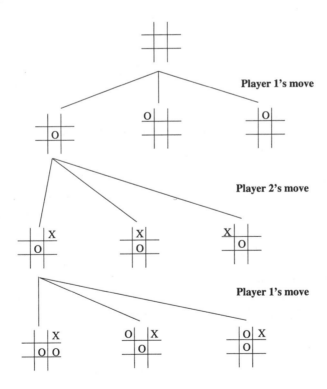

Figure 4.12 *Partial Game Tree for Noughts and Crosses.*

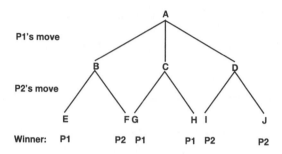

Figure 4.13 *Game Tree for Simple Game.*

represented by the letters A–J rather than a picture of an actual board.) How should player 1 decide which move to make? Each player should obviously assume that the other will try to win. If player 1 moves to state B, then player 2 will choose to move to state F, and so win. If player 1 moves to state C, any move player 2 attempts will still result in player 1 winning. If player 1 moves to state D, any move player 2 makes will result in player 2 winning. Clearly the only safe move for player 1 is to state C.

The Minimax Procedure

For a complete game tree like this, we can find good moves for the first player as follows. First, we'll say that an eventual win for player 1 will be indicated by a positive score of 10, a lose by a negative score −10 and a draw by 0. Then we can work bottom up and work out the scores of earlier nodes in the game tree. Figure 4.14 has these intermediate scores indicated for another simple game tree. At nodes E, F, G and H it is player 1's turn to move. He will try to *maximize* his score. From nodes E, F and H he has a winning move, so these nodes are scored 10. From node G he can at best draw, so this node is scored 0. Now, at nodes B and C it is player 2's move, and player 2 will try to *minimize* player 1's score. (Nodes B and C are referred to as minimizing nodes, while E-H are maximizing nodes.) At node B, whatever player 2 does player 1 has a winning move. The score there is the *minimum* of the scores at nodes E and F, but this is still 10. At node C the minimum score is 0, corresponding to player 2's option of moving to node G and forcing player 1 into a no-win situation. So, player 1 can now reliably say that node B corresponds to the best move, and that from there he has a guaranteed win.

The procedure for assigning a score to a node is as follows:

To score(node):

- If node is at leaf of search tree, return score of that node
- else if it is a maximizing node then return maximum of scores of successor nodes

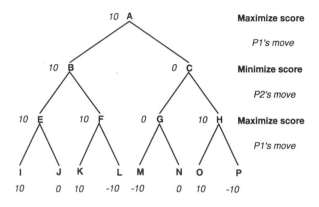

Figure 4.14 *Game Tree Illustrating Minimax.*

- else if it is a minimizing node then return minimum of scores of successor nodes

Player 1 will select which move to make after scoring the possible moves as described above. This is referred to as the *minimax procedure* for game playing. You should go through how this would work for the noughts and crosses example. To keep things simple, imagine that you are half-way through a game, and deciding where to put the next cross. Draw the game tree for the rest of the game, and show how minimax would allow you to determine the best move.

Alpha-Beta Pruning

There is a very simple trick that significantly increases the efficiency of the minimax procedure. It is based on the idea that if you know half-way through a calculation that it will succeed or fail, then there is no point doing the rest of it. For example, in programming languages it is clear that when evaluating statements like if A>5 or B<0, then if the first condition succeeds there is no need to bother trying the second. Or for if A>5 and B<0 there is no point continuing if the first condition *fails*.

I'll start by illustrating the technique using Figure 4.14. Suppose the score for node B has been found. As player 1 will be *maximizing* his score, then we know that he can get *at least* a score of 10 without even examining node C. So the score for node A is at least 10. Suppose the score of node G has also been found. Player 2 will be *minimizing* player 1's score, so the score for node C can be *at most* 0. Taken together, these mean that there is no point working out the score for node H, as there is no way it can affect the score of node A. Suppose node H's score was less than zero. This would change the score of node C, but node A can still get a score of 10, so is unchanged. Suppose node H's score was greater than (or equal to) zero. Node C's score would be unchanged, and hence also node A's. This example is illustrated slightly more simply in Figure 4.15. The score of node H makes no

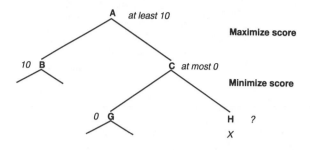

Figure 4.15 *Game Tree Illustrating Alpha-Beta Pruning.*

difference, so the part of the tree below that node (marked X) can be completely ignored.

Alpha-beta pruning involves keeping track of the *at most* and *at least* values, and using these to make savings like that illustrated above. We know that the score at a *maximizing* node is going to be at least the best score of the successor nodes examined so far (a parameter α is used to record this). The score at a *minimizing* node is going to be at most the worst score of the successor nodes examined so far (a parameter β is used for this). If the β value of a minimizing node is less than the α value of its parent node then all remaining calculations on that node can be abandoned. The rest of the tree is *pruned*. If the α value of a maximizing node is greater than the β value of its parent, similarly the rest of the calculations on a node can be abandoned, or the tree pruned.

Alpha-beta pruning is just used to make the minimax procedure more efficient. It has been described rather briefly here, but this should be sufficient for you to work through some examples and see how it would work out in practice.

More Complex Games

For more complex or sophisticated games it is, in fact, not realistic to work out the complete game tree, even with alpha-beta pruning. For chess, there are billions of possible board states. However, a variant of the above method can be used. We limit the *depth* that is explored in the search tree (to, say, five moves ahead), and for the board states corresponding to the leaves in the limited search tree (which may or may not be winning states), a heuristic scoring function is used to assign a score to the node. For chess, a simple score might correspond to a points score of the player's remaining pieces. The above scoring function is then used to determine the scores of nodes further up the tree, so that the player can select the best move. For chess, and assuming a score based on remaining pieces, and a five-move depth limit, this corresponds to a strategy of looking for a move that is guaranteed to at least gain you piece advantage in the move, by five moves ahead. This may not guarantee a winning game (sometimes you have to sacrifice pieces to do better later on), but it may be moderately effective.

Using these fairly straightforward (and not terribly intelligent) techniques for game playing systems results in pretty good performance. However, for even better performance it is necessary to look a bit at how human experts play a game. For example, in chess opening and closing moves are very important, and there are some fairly standard opening games. Enhancing a search-based system with knowledge of these good opening and closing sequences (as you might find in any chess book) should improve its performance.

4.4 Summary

- Solving many AI problems involves using *search* techniques. For example, in simple state-space search we may search through possible sequences of actions to find one that will achieve a target state, from some initial one. A particular state that we can reach from the initial one would be a *node* in the *search space*, and the sequence of actions would be a *path*.

- The search space may be a *tree* or a general *graph*. Different algorithms involve *traversing* this search space in a different manner.

- The simplest search methods are *breadth first* and *depth first*. These involve exhaustively traversing the search space in a systematic manner. In breadth first, short paths are searched before longer ones. In depth first, a path is searched to its end before backing up and trying alternatives.

- *Heuristic* search methods attempt to use some knowledge of how close a state is to a target state to select which paths to explore first. This may avoid the whole search space being searched, resulting in a faster solution. Hill climbing, best first and A* are all heuristic search methods.

- More sophisticated *planning* techniques are often required to solve problems. AI planning systems use a more complex representation of actions than simple search-based problem solvers. Simple planning algorithms control the search through possible actions by looking for actions that reduce the *difference* between current and target states, and by setting new subproblems to solve if a useful action cannot be applied in the current state.

- Search techniques may also be applied to game playing systems, but here you have to take into account what the opponent might do. The *minimax* procedure allows you to find the best move, assuming that the opponent will do his best to prevent you winning.

4.5   Further Reading

Most of the longer AI textbooks have good sections on search, game playing and planning, including more complex approaches and more mathematical analysis. Discussions of search methods tend to be similar in different books, but details of planning algorithms and representations tend to differ. Rich & Knight (Rich & Knight, 1991) (chs.2–3, 12–13) discuss more problem-solving methods, and include discussion of the benefits of the alternative approaches. Ginsberg (Ginsberg, 1993) (chs.3–5, 14) provides complexity analysis of algorithms, and a logic-based approach to planning. Russell & Norvig (Russell & Norvig, 1995) (chs.3–5, 11–13) have a very clear discussion of basic state-space search and search algorithms, and more modern planning systems. Luger & Stubblefield (Luger & Stubblefield, 1993) (chs.3–5) provide a more implementation-oriented discussion.

4.6   Exercises

1. Given the following search tree, state the order in which the nodes will be searched for breadth first, depth first, hill climbing, and best first search, until a solution is reached. The numbers on the nodes indicate the estimated cost to solution.

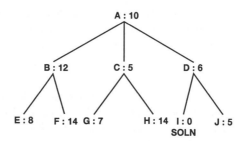

2. The following is a problem which can be solved using state-space search techniques:

> "A farmer with his dog, rabbit and lettuce come to the east side of a river they wish to cross. There is a boat at the river's edge, but of course only the farmer can row. The boat can only hold two things (including the rower) at any one time. If the dog is ever left alone with the rabbit, the dog will eat it. Similarly if the rabbit is ever left alone with the lettuce, the rabbit will eat it. How can the farmer get across the river so that the dog, rabbit and lettuce arrive safely on the other side?"

Formalise the above problem in terms of state-space search. You should:

- Suggest a suitable representation for the problem state.

- State what the initial and final states are in this representation.

- State the available operators/rules for getting from one state to the next, giving any conditions on when they may be applied.

3. For the following problem, first discuss how it could be solved using simple state-space search techniques, then discuss how it could be solved using the simple planning methods introduced in Section 4.3.2. Compare and contrast the two methods.

   "You live in a two room house with one door between the rooms. Your robot can move between rooms, turn around (by $180°$), open the door, and pick objects up. You want him to be able to form plans to do simple tasks, like get your beer from the other room and bring it to you. To move between rooms the door has to be open, and to open a door the robot has to be facing towards it."

4. Why does depth first search require less memory than breadth first? Consider the case where the search space is uniform with every node having two successors, to a depth of eight, and estimate the number of nodes that will be on the agenda for each method when the current node is a leaf node.

5. (Project) Try implementing the minimax game playing procedure. Use it for a simple noughts and crosses game.

CHAPTER 5

Natural Language Processing

Aims: To introduce the basics of natural language process-
                 ing, focusing on writing simple *grammars* using def-
                 inite clause grammar (DCG) notation.

Objectives: You should be able to:
                 Briefly describe the main stages of processing in nat-
                 ural language understanding, including speech pro-
                 cessing, syntactic analysis, semantics and pragmat-
                 ics.
                 Develop (or extend) a simple grammar of English,
                 using DCG notation.

Prerequisites: The following would be useful, although not essen-
                 tial: knowledge of syntactic categories (noun, verb,
                 etc.); knowledge of BNF (grammar) notation; a basic
                 knowledge of Prolog.

5.1   Introduction

The next two chapters are concerned with two "mundane" tasks: natural language
and vision. Both of these are tasks that humans can do very easily – even a small
child can recognize a face or take part in a conversation – yet the tasks are very
difficult to automate.

Natural language processing can be divided into natural language *understanding* and natural language *generation*. Natural language understanding involves taking some spoken or typed sentence and working out what it means, so that something can be done with it. Natural language generation is concerned with the opposite: taking some formal representation of what you want to say and working out a

way to express it in English (or some other *natural*[1] language). This chapter will be primarily concerned with natural language understanding, with the goal of finding the meaning of an English sentence.

Natural language systems are developed both to explore general theories of human language processing and to do practical tasks such as providing natural language interfaces or front ends to application systems. In the latter case the job of the understanding system is to interpet the user's utterances and translate them into a suitable form for the application. For example, for a natural language front end to a database system the goal might be to translate an English sentence into a formal database query.

In general the user might want to communicate with a system by speaking or by typing. Understanding spoken language is much harder than understanding typed language – the input is just the raw speech signals taken from a microphone. Before we can get to work on what the speech means we must work out from the speech signal what words are being spoken. This is referred to as *speech recognition*. This is the first stage of language understanding, and the output is the sequence of words spoken.

Once this sequence of words has been obtained, the rest of the understanding process can be divided into further stages: syntactic analysis, semantic analysis and pragmatics. Along with speech recognition this gives the following four stages of natural language understanding, also illustrated in Figure 5.1.

Speech Recognition: The raw speech signal is analysed and the sequence of words spoken is obtained.

Syntactic Analysis: The sequence of words spoken is analysed using knowledge of the *grammar* of the language and the *structure* of the sentence is obtained.

Semantic Analysis: Using information about the structure of the sentence and the meaning of the words in it, a partial representation of the meaning of the whole sentence is obtained.

Pragmatic Analysis: Finally, this partial representation of what the sentence means is filled in using information about the *context*, that is, things like when and where it was said and who was saying it to whom.

Other books may list slightly different stages. However, it is generally accepted that some such division of the understanding task is useful.

In the rest of this chapter we'll first go through each of these stages of language understanding, with most emphasis on *syntactic analysis*. This will be followed by a discussion of the problem of *ambiguity* in language. Finally we'll return to look briefly at the other side of language processing, *generation*.

---

[1]The term *natural* language is used to distinguish natural human languages such as English, Japanese, etc. from formal languages such as computer programming languages and logic.

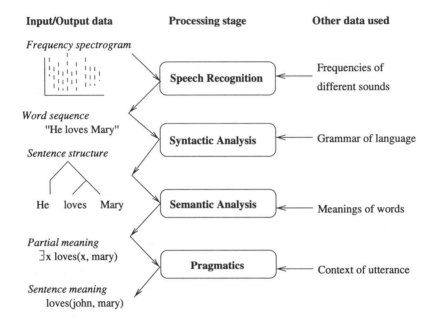

Figure 5.1 *Stages of Natural Language Understanding.*

5.2   Speech Recognition

Speech recognition is the process where a speech signal is analysed and the sequence of words spoken obtained. If that sequence of words is further analysed to obtain its meaning, as discussed in the later sections, then we refer to the whole process as *speech understanding.*

   Speech understanding is hard. Yet the prospect of being able to communicate with a computer through everyday speech is a very attractive one; you don't find Captain Kirk[2] *typing* on *Star Trek.* Speech input allows flexible input without requiring typing skills, over the telephone where necessary, at high speeds, and leaving hands free for other things. It may be some way into the future before we can talk to our computer, on any topic, and have it understand and respond to us. But even limited speech understanding is useful, and restricted speech understanding systems are in everyday practical use.

5.2.1   An Outline of the Speech Recognition Process

Figure 5.2 illustrates how the *frequency spectrogram* is obtained, which is the starting point for our analysis. Output from a microphone is an *analog signal*, which can be split up into different *frequencies* using special filters. This is like

---

[2]Or, indeed, that recent upstart, Jean Luc Picard.

Figure 5.2 *Speech Signal.*

dividing up a sound into parts that are high pitched and parts that are low pitched. At a given time the amount of energy in each frequency can be measured. This is plotted on a frequency spectrogram which gives, for each point in time, the quantity of each frequency of interest. (In the figure, the bold line segments are meant to crudely illustrate where there might be a lot of a given frequency at the given time.)

Having obtained the frequency spectrogram, the next thing is to find out what word it might correspond to. This is split into two main stages. The first stage is to guess what basic *sounds* occur in the signal. All human languages use a small number (40–50) of basic sounds called *phonemes*. These are things like the "a" sound in "cat" and the "sh" sound in "shopping". We can easily obtain a complete library giving frequency spectrograms (*templates*) for each phoneme. Now, if we have a new spectrogram corresponding to a fragment of speech we can find out which phonemes are being uttered by a process of matching fragments of the given spectrogram with ones in the library, looking for the best match. This is referred to as *template matching*. It may involve a process called *dynamic time warping* which allows a good match to be found even if the two sounds were spoken at different speeds.

The next stage involves taking these phonemes and working out what word(s) they correspond to. For example, we might take the phonemes "th", "i" and "ng" and deduce that the word is "thing". If the previous stage was reliable, and if a given word was always pronounced in the same way, then this would be just a straightforward lookup and match with the phonetic spelling of dictionary words. However, obtaining the phonemes from the speech signals tends to be very unreliable, for all sorts of reasons to be discussed next. So after the first stage the results might be just probabilities for different possible phonemes based on goodness of match. Maybe there's a 50% chance that it's a "th" sound, but 30% that it's a "f" sound. Things can be complicated further by the fact that a given word can often be pronounced in a number of different ways (e.g., tomato).

Finding which word was spoken (or at least, the most likely one) therefore involves using all sorts of *statistical* information. This includes the likelihoods of the possible phonemes, the likelihoods of the different pronunciations, and also the likelihoods of the words themselves. The likelihood of a given word in turn depends

Practical Applications

Simple speech recognizers are in fairly widespread use, particularly for telephone applications. For example, one American telephone company uses speech recognition to handle collect (reverse charge) calls and other services. The system asks for and records the caller's name and dials the number, and then asks the person called whether they'll accept the charges. It then has to determine simply whether the reply is yes or no (or a variant of these, such as "OK, sure"). If it can't determine this it can pass control back to a human operator. This system obviously needs only a small vocabulary, but must be speaker-independent. It uses a number of templates to capture all the different pronunciations of yes, no, and variants.

Speech recognition systems are also in use for telephone banking services. Again, typically a very small vocabulary is allowed, such as the digits zero to nine, yes, no etc. The dialogue with the user must be very focused or *channelled* to ensure the user answers in one of the expected ways.

---

on what word or words occurred before it (e.g., "the" is unlikely to occur after "a"). The methods used to find out the probabilities of different words involve a statistical technique called *hidden Markov modelling*. These statistical methods, which are too complex to discuss here, have been very successful in speech recognition.

5.2.2 Problems and Complications

The main problem in speech recognition is that there is no simple mapping from speech signal to word. The same word may be pronounced in many different ways by different speakers, particularly if they have different dialects or are of a different sex. Even the same speaker will pronounce things slightly differently on different occasions, speaking fast or slowly, with varied intonation. The same sound may also correspond to several possible words (e.g., bear and bare).

As there are often virtually no gaps between words in normal speech it may also be hard to work out where one word ends and another begins. A famous example of this is the utterance "How to recognize speech" which can sound pretty much the same as "How to wreck a nice beach"! Background noise may also complicate things: we might have to separate the signals resulting from the wind whistling in the trees or the telephone ringing in the background from the signals resulting from Fred saying "Hello". If the words are spoken over the telephone there are yet further problems. High frequencies may be removed by the telephone system, and as a result certain phonemes (such as "f" and "s") sound just the same.

Because of all these problems, speech recognition systems often make one or more of a number of simplifying assumptions. The first is that they will only ever be dealing with a *single speaker*. This contrasts with *speaker independent* systems, which are meant to handle any speaker. In a single speaker system the templates used for phoneme matching can come from that very speaker. The speaker will *train* the system by uttering some specified sounds or words, and these are used in recognition.

Another simplifying assumption is that the input consists of one word at a time, with significant pauses between words. *Individual word recognizers* deal with such input. *Continuous speech recognizers* attempt to deal with normal continuous speech without the pauses.

Speech recognition is also simpler if we are dealing with a *restricted vocabulary*. As an extreme example, a useful system might just be able to distinguish between the words "yes" and "no", or the digits zero to nine. Finally, a speech system may assume that the speaker is working in a quiet environment, with no significant noise.

A speech recognition system might be described as, for example, a "speaker independent, continuous speech system with a vocabulary of 500 words". Current state of the art systems of this kind (i.e., fairly general-purpose systems, with few simplifying assumptions) might get around 80–90% of words right. This isn't really good enough for practical applications today. Systems that make more simplifying assumptions may be more accurate, and be of more current practical use.

5.2.3 Speech Understanding

The output of a speech recognizer is just a sequence or sequences of words, perhaps with probabilities indicating which of a number of possible sequences is more likely. For some applications, that word sequence is all that is needed. For example, a telephone system might just want to determine whether the speaker said "yes" or "no" after a question, and take different action according to which it was. Or an automatic dictation program might just output the text, to be processed in a word processor.

However, for more interesting applications we need to work out what the sequence of words means. For this we need the next stages of natural language understanding, discussed below[3].

---

[3]In fact the way natural language understanding proceeds may be slightly different if the input is speech data, due to the uncertainties in the data and the fact that speech is often not *grammatical*. However, to simplify things we'll assume that conventional language processing methods are used.

5.3 Syntactic Analysis

Syntactic analysis helps us understand how words are grouped together to make complex sentences, and gives us a starting point for working out the meaning of the whole sentence. For example, consider the following two sentences:

(1) The dog ate the bone.
(2) The bone was eaten by the dog.

Understanding the *structure* of the sentence, via the rules of syntax, help us work out that it's the bone that gets eaten and not the dog. A simple rule like "it's the second noun that gets eaten" just won't work.

Syntactic analysis allows us to determine possible groupings of words in a sentence. Sometimes there will only be one possible grouping, and we will be well on the way to working out the meaning. For example, in the following sentence:

(3) The rabbit with long ears enjoyed a large green lettuce.

we can work out from the rules of syntax that "the rabbit with long ears" forms one group (a noun phrase), and "a large green lettuce" forms another noun phrase group. When we get to work on determining the meaning of the sentence, we can start off by working out the meaning of these word groups, before combining them together to get the meaning of the whole sentence.

In other cases there may be many possible groupings of words. For example, for the sentence "John saw Mary with a telescope" there are two different readings based on the following groupings:

(4i) John saw (Mary with a telescope). i.e., John saw Mary who is holding a telescope.
(4ii) John (saw Mary with a telescope). i.e., John looked at her through a telescope.

When there are many possible groupings then the sentence is syntactically ambiguous. Sometimes we will be able to use general knowledge to work out which is the intended grouping – for example, consider the following sentence:

(5) I saw the Forth bridge flying into Edinburgh.

There are two possible readings, one involving the speaker flying (presumably in an aeroplane) and looking down at the bridge, and the other involving the bridge flying. We can probably guess that the Forth bridge isn't flying! So, this sentence is *syntactically ambiguous*, but unambiguous if we bring to bear general knowledge about bridges. In example (4) general knowledge alone is insufficient to work out the intended meaning. However, if we know something about John and Mary (e.g.,

John is in the habit of looking at girls through a telescope) we can again guess at the intended meaning. This is discussed further in Section 5.6.

Syntactic analysis clearly helps a lot in determining the meaning of a sentence by working out possible structures (basically, word groupings). As discussed above, there may be alternative structures, and the right one (i.e., the one intended by the speaker or writer) may only be determined using additional information. However, it is generally best to start with the syntax, and the rest of this section will consider how such analysis is done.

5.3.1 Writing a Grammar

Rules of syntax specify the possible organizations of words in sentences, and allow us to determine a particular sentence's structure (or possible structures) and hence help determine its meaning. They are specified by writing a *grammar* for the language. To analyse the structure of a sentence we also need a *parser*, which, given a sentence (or sequence of "symbols") and a grammar, will check that the sentence is correct according to the grammar, and if so return a representation of the sentence's structure. The structure is normally returned as a *parse tree* for the sentence, indicating the possible groupings of words into higher-level syntactic constituents. This section will describe how simple grammars may be written, focusing on the definite clause grammar (DCG) formalism which can be handled very straightforwardly in the Prolog language. The following section will discuss more briefly the parsing process.

A natural language grammar specifies allowable sentence structures in terms of basic syntactic categories such as nouns and verbs. It is defined in a similar way to a grammar for a programming language, but will need to be more complex. Because of the complexity of natural language a given grammar is unlikely to cover all possible grammatical sentences.

In natural language we don't usually parse language in order to check that it is "correct". We parse it in order to determine the structure and help work out the meaning. But most grammars are just concerned with the structure of grammatically correct English, as it gets much more complex to parse if you allow ungrammatical English. It is also easier to introduce grammars by just considering how to write a grammar that will "recognize" grammatically correct sentences, but fail to recognize incorrect sentences. The problem of returning the structure can be left until later.

A starting point for describing the structure of a natural language is to use a simple *context free* grammar (as often used to describe the syntax of programming languages). Suppose we want a grammar that will recognize sentences like the following:

1. John ate the biscuit.
2. The lion ate the schizophrenic.
3. The lion kissed John.

```
sentence  --> noun_phrase, verb_phrase.
noun_phrase --> proper_noun.
noun_phrase --> determiner, noun.
verb_phrase --> verb, noun_phrase.

proper_noun --> [mary].
proper_noun --> [john].
noun --> [schizophrenic].
noun --> [biscuit].
verb --> [ate].
verb --> [kissed].
determiner --> [the].
```

Figure 5.3 *A Simple Grammar of English.*

but will fail to recognize incorrect sentences like:

1. Ate John biscuit the.
2. Schizophrenic the lion the ate.
3. Biscuit lion kissed.

A simple grammar that deals with this is given in Figure 5.3. The notation used is the definite clause grammar (DCG) formalism, or specifically Prolog's DCG notation. This is basically a variant of BNF notations, often used to describe the syntax of programming languages (the symbols : : =, or just = are sometimes used in BNF in place of - ->, but mean just the same). The first rule says that a sentence *consists of* a noun phrase and a verb phrase. The noun phrase corresponds to the *subject* of the sentence – the thing that does something. The verb phrase corresponds to the *predicate* – the thing that was done. So, in the sentence "John ate the biscuit", "John" is the noun phrase (John does something) and "ate the biscuit" is the verb phrase (that's what he does).

The remaining rules can be read as follows. A noun phrase consists of either a proper noun (using the second rule) *or* a determiner (a word like "the" or "a") followed by a noun. A verb phrase consists of a verb (e.g., ate) and a noun phrase.

The rules at the end are really like dictionary entries, which state the syntactic category of different words. The format given for these (i.e., in square brackets) is the simplest way of expressing such entries when using Prolog's DCG formalism.

Considering further the example sentences above, the sentence "John ate the biscuit" consists of a noun phrase "John" and a verb phrase "ate the biscuit". The noun phrase is just a proper noun, while the verb phrase consists of a verb "ate" and another noun phrase ("the biscuit"). This noun phrase consists of a determiner "the" and a noun "biscuit". The incorrect sentences will be excluded by the grammar. For example, "biscuit lion kissed" starts with two nouns, which is not allowed in the grammar. However, some odd sentences will be allowed, such as "The biscuit kissed John". This sentence is syntactically acceptable, just semantically odd, so should still be recognized by the grammar.

For a given grammar we can illustrate the syntactic structure of the sentence by giving the *parse tree*, which shows how the sentence is broken down into different syntactic constituents. This kind of information may be useful for later semantic processing. Figure 5.4 illustrates the parse tree for "John ate the lion", given the grammar in Figure 5.3. In the next section we will look at how such parse trees can be returned using a DCG grammar in Prolog.

The grammar given above is, of course, very limited. It will fail to handle complex sentences (such as this one), yet it will recognize some sentences that we might regard as clearly ungrammatical. Consider the following two sentences:

- Mary eat the lion.
- Mary eats the ferocious lion.

If "eat" and "eats" are categorized as verbs then, given the simple grammar above, the first sentence will be acceptable according to the grammar, while the second won't – there is no mention of adjectives in our grammar. Yet the first should NOT be accepted, as it should be "eats" rather than "eat" in order to get subject–verb number agreement right. The second sentence should obviously be accepted. To deal with the first problem we need to have some method of enforcing number agreement between subjects and verbs, so that things like "I am..." and

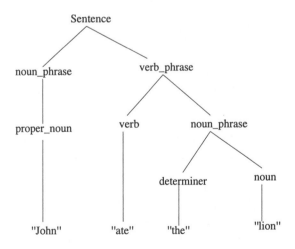

Figure 5.4 *Parse Tree for "John ate the lion".*

```
sentence --> noun_phrase(Num), verb_phrase(Num).
noun_phrase(Num) --> proper_noun(Num).
noun_phrase(Num) --> determiner(Num), noun(Num).
verb_phrase(Num) --> verb(Num), noun_phrase(_).

proper_noun(s) --> [mary].
noun(s) --> [lion].
noun(p) --> [lions].
det(s) --> [the].
det(p) --> [the].
verb(s) --> [eats].
verb(p) --> [eat].
```

Figure 5.5 *A Simple Grammar with Subject–Verb Number Agreement.*

"We are..." are accepted, but "I are..." and "We am..." are not. To deal with the second problem we need to add further rules to our grammar.

To enforce subject–verb agreement the simplest method is to add arguments to the grammar rules. This strictly means that the grammar is no longer 'context free', but this is permitted in the DCG formalism. If we're only concerned about singular versus plural nouns we might get the rules and dictionary entries given in Figure 5.5. For those unfamiliar with Prolog, capital letters indicate *variables*, so Num is a variable, while s denotes a specific entity, in this case a singular noun or verb. Here Num refers the *number* of a noun or verb which can be singular (s) or plural (p).

The grammar can be read as follows. A sentence consists of a noun phrase and a verb phrase, both of which have an associated number Num, which should be the same. A noun phrase with an associated number consists either of a proper noun or a determiner and noun, all with the relevant number. A verb phrase consists of a verb of the specified number, plus a noun phrase. This latter noun phrase does NOT have to agree with the number of the verb (consider "John eats the carrot" and "John eats the carrots"). This is therefore indicated using a "_" symbol which should be familiar to Prolog programmers, but which can be viewed here as a "don't care" symbol. Finally, each of the dictionary entries has its number specified as s or p.

In general, getting agreement right in a grammar is much more complex than this. We need both fairly complex rules, and also to put more information in dictionary entries. A good dictionary will not state everything explicitly, but will exploit general information about word structure, such as the fact that, given a verb such as "eat" the third person singular form generally involves adding an "s": hit/hits, eat/eats, like/likes etc. *Morphology* is the area of natural language processing concerned with the structure of words.

To extend the grammar to allow adjectives we need to add an extra rule or two, e.g.,

```
noun_phrase(Num) -->
    determiner(Num), adjectives, noun(Num).
adjectives --> [].
adjectives --> adjective, adjectives.

adjective --> [ferocious].
adjective --> [ugly].
```

That is, noun phrases can consist of a determiner, some adjectives and a noun. Adjectives can consist of either nothing at all (they are optional), or an adjective and some more adjectives. Putting this all together we can now parse the sentence "the ferocious ugly lion eats Mary", and similar.

Note that the adjective rule is *recursive* (i.e., refers to itself). It allows any number of adjectives, from none to an infinite list. Logically we could also have written the rule as: `adjectives --> adjectives, adjective`. However, that would be *left recursive* and most simple parsers would not be able to cope with it, going into an infinite loop. Exactly the same problem occurs when writing recursive functions or procedures in most programming languages, so it should be a familiar problem to programmers.

So far, starting from a very simple grammar, we have shown how it can be extended to deal with slightly more complex sentences or grammatical constraints. To illustrate some further simple ways a grammar can be extended, consider the following sentence: "The man with the hairy beard dubiously eats the beef that Europe rejects." First, a grammar must deal with *adjectives* like "hairy" and *adverbs* like "dubiously". Next, it must deal with *prepositional phrases* such as "with the hairy beard" that *modify* a noun phrase by adding some extra information about it. Also, *relative clauses* such as "that Europe rejects" must be handled; relative clauses also modify a noun phrase. This particular relative clause is a complex one involving a phenomenon called *filler gap dependency*. It is not important now to understand all these terms, just to appreciate the complexity that may be required.

Even this fairly simple and artificially constructed sentence requires a moderately complex grammar to allow it to be correctly recognized. To cover more complex sentences, such as the ones in this paragraph, it would have to be extended much further, possibly using a more sophisticated grammatical formalism. A grammar covering a significant portion of English might consist of hundreds of rules.

One final point should be made before leaving this section. At the beginning of the section we mentioned that the purpose of syntactic analysis was to determine the structure it assigns to the sentence so that this structure could aid in working out the meaning of the sentence. This initial goal has been somewhat lost in talking about how to write a grammar to ensure that correct sentences are recognized and incorrect ones rejected. A grammar should *also* ensure that the structure of the sentence is sensible, grouping associated words together. The following grammar fragment, for example, while accepting similar sentences to the grammar in Figure 5.3, does not result in associated words being grouped together:

```
sentence --> det, nounverbdet, noun.
nounverbdet --> noun, verb, det.
```

In the sentence "The dog ate the lion" the grouping with this grammar is "The (dog ate the) lion" while in the grammar in Figure 5.3 it is "(The dog) (ate (the lion))" which I hope you can see is more sensible. Each bracketed section is meaningful (to some extent) by itself. This feature makes it much easier to use this structure to find the meaning of the whole sentence by looking at the meaning of individual parts of the sentence. This will be discussed in more detail in Section 5.4.

5.3.2 Parsing

Having a grammar isn't enough to parse natural language – you need a parser. The parser should search for possible ways the rules of the grammar can be used to parse the sentence; parsing can be viewed as a kind of search problem[4]. In general there may be many different rules that can be used to "expand" or *rewrite* a given syntactic category, and the parser must check through them all, to see if the sentence can be parsed using any combination of them. For example, in our mini-grammar above there were two rules for noun_phrases; a parse of the noun phrase may use either one or the other.

So, to parse a sentence we need to search through all these possibilities, effectively going through all possible syntactic structures to find one that fits the sentence. There are many ways of doing this, varying in complexity and efficiency. One way is basically to do a depth first search through the parse tree, backtracking when a word in the sentence fails to match the syntactic category expected. This method is built into the Prolog language, which means that when using DCGs in Prolog there is no need for a separate parser. In fact, DCGs are just translated by the Prolog system into ordinary Prolog, and the normal Prolog backtracking mechanism used to parse a sentence.

The grammars listed in Figures 5.3 and 5.5 can be used directly as Prolog programs, with no additions, to determine whether a sentence is syntactically acceptable according to the grammar. However, the result, as is so common with Prolog programs, is just "yes" or "no". This may be useful if you want to check the grammatical correctness of a sentence but is of little use when trying to work out what that sentence means. To do this there are two alternative approaches that can be taken. The first is to *combine* semantic with syntactic analysis. This will be

---

[4]While computer language grammars can be (re)written in such a way as to avoid the need for search in the parsing process, natural languages cannot. So the parsers are often a bit more complex.

discussed further in Section 5.4, but the idea is that the meaning of a sentence is put together at the same time as the structure is analysed, composed from the meanings of the parts which are grouped together according to syntax. The second approach is to return the *parse tree* (referred to above) and use that to guide a separate stage of semantic analysis. This will be discussed a little here.

The parse tree should reflect the structure of the sentence according to the grammar. The example in Figure 5.4 illustrated this. The top symbol in the parse tree will be `sentence`. According to the grammar, a sentence can consist of a noun phrase and a verb phrase, so this is indicated by the relevant branches of the tree. A noun phrase can consist of a proper noun or a determiner and a noun. For the first word "John" the first case applies, while for "the lion" the second case applies. These choices are reflected in the tree. Figure 5.6 illustrates a slightly more complex parse tree; this will also serve as a useful hint for Exercise 5.1.

Although a graphical representation of a parse tree is good for visualizing it, the information about the tree structure can be represented textually. The following structure (which can, conveniently, be manipulated directly in Prolog) captures the tree structure in Figure 5.4 (using abbreviations for sentence, noun phrase, etc.):

```
s(np(pn(john)), vp(v(ate), np(d(the),n(lion))))
```

It turns out that it is possible to construct such structures very straightforwardly in Prolog's DCG notation simply by adding an additional argument to every term. This additional argument is used to build up a structure like the above. This is illustrated in the rule below. However, for full details you should consult a Prolog text – most will discuss this.

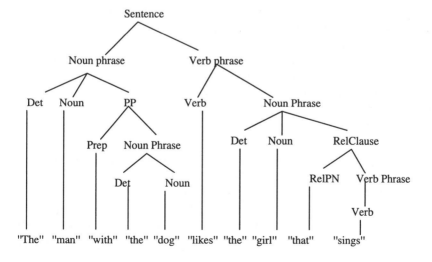

Figure 5.6 *Another Parse Tree.*

```
noun_phrase(np(DetTree, NounTree)) -->
    determiner(DetTree),
    noun(NounTree).


noun(n(banana)) --> [banana].
```

It is very easy to write grammars as DCGs and to use Prolog's built-in back-tracking mechanism for parsing. We can even get all possible parses through back-tracking. However, it is also easy to write a very inefficient system in this way. What tends to happen is that successfully parsed fragments get thrown away when backtracking occurs, and the parsing has to be redone. Other parsing methods may try to avoid this. For example, a *chart* parser explicitly records in a special data structure called a chart all the possible parses of each bit of the sentence, so they never get thrown away. To find out about other parsing methods you should consult some of the further reading mentioned at the end of the chapter.

5.4   Semantics

The remaining two stages of analysis, semantics and pragmatics, are concerned with getting at the *meaning* of a sentence. In the first stage (semantics) a partial representation of the meaning is obtained based on the possible syntactic structure(s) of the sentence, and on the meanings of the words in that sentence. In the second stage (pragmatics), the meaning is elaborated based on *contextual* and world knowledge.

A goal of semantic interpretation is to find a way that the meaning of the whole sentence can be put together in a simple way from the meaning of the parts of the sentence. This is referred to as *compositional semantics* . It may not always be possible, but if it is possible it makes life much simpler[5]. The division of the sentence into meaningful parts is that provided by syntactic analysis.

In general the meaning of a sentence may be represented in many ways, using any of the knowledge representation schemes mentioned in Chapter 2. For practical applications the meaning might be represented as, say, a database query, using a particular query language. However, in this section we'll assume that the meaning is to be represented in predicate logic. This is not adequate for representing arbitrary English sentences, and may not be the best choice for some applications, but it allows the key ideas to be presented quite simply.

In predicate logic we represent a sentence like "John loves Mary" straightforwardly as $loves(john, mary)$. Here the symbols $john$ and $mary$ refer to specific entities. For a sentence like "The man likes Mary" we don't (yet) know which

---

[5]Note that this is not the only approach to semantic interpretation. See the further reading at the end of the chapter.

man it is, so it is necessary to invent a symbol for this hypothetical man – say $m1$ – giving semantics $man(m1) \land likes(mary, m1)$. If we have "a man likes Mary" then there isn't necessarily even any specific man in mind, so this can be represented as $\exists x(man(x) \land likes(x, mary))$. If the sentence contains adjectives things get more complex again; "A tall bearded man likes Mary" has semantics $\exists x(man(x) \land tall(x) \land bearded(x) \land likes(x, mary))$. If we try to represent sentences like the ones in this paragraph then things get very complex indeed, and predicate logic is unlikely to be adequate.

Anyway, to illustrate compositional semantics we will start with the simplest possible example "John jumps" and progress to "John loves Mary". More complex examples are given in (Pereira & Shieber, 1987).

Compositional semantics requires some way of representing each word in the sentence such that they can be combined in a systematic manner to find the meaning of the whole. Representing "John" is easy; we just use the symbol $john$. Representing "jumps" is a little harder. To do compositional semantics we don't need to know that "jumps" means leaping upwards. We just need to represent somehow that "jumps" is a verb that takes a 'subject' (something or someone doing the jumping) in such a way that when combined with the jumper we get an expression like $jumps(john)$ or $jumps(mary)$.

One way to do this is to represent "jumps" as a predicate with one variable argument: $jumps(X)$. The question now is how can you combine this expression with $john$ to give $jumps(john)$.

Figure 5.7 illustrates how the ideas discussed so far could be realized as a DCG. The semantics of a given syntactic category are given as arguments. The first rule just says that a sentence consists of a noun phrase and a verb phrase, and the meaning of the sentence is obtained by combining the meaning of the noun phrase with the meaning of the verb phrase. The question then becomes, how can we combine these parts?

To do this for our example we need some way of getting at the argument X

```
sentence(SMeaning) -->
    noun_phrase(NPMeaning), verb_phrase(VPMeaning),
    combine(NPMeaning, VPMeaning, SMeaning).

noun_phrase(NPMeaning) --> proper_noun(NPMeaning).

verb_phrase(VPMeaning) --> verb(VPMeaning).

proper_noun(john) --> [john].
verb(jumps(X)) --> [jumps].
verb(cries(X)) --> [cries].
```

Figure 5.7 *A Simple Grammar with Semantics: Initial Version.*

of $jumps(X)$ so that we can set its value to $john$. In Prolog a good way to do
this, in a way that will work for other examples, is to use a slightly more complex
structure that has the relevant argument stuck on the front. One possibility is to
make it $X\hat{\ }jumps(X)$. (The $\hat{\ }$ symbol is arbitrary – it's just there to separate the
X from the $jumps(X)$.) With this slightly more complex representation of verb
meaning we can implement a combine predicate as follows:

```
combine(NPMeaning, VPMeaning, SMeaning) :-
    VPMeaning = Arg^Expr,
    Arg = NPMeaning,
    SMeaning = Expr.
```

For those familiar with Prolog, this can be done even more simply. You should
consider how. For those not familiar with Prolog this just splits up the verb phrase
meaning into the argument and the main expression (e.g., X and jumps(X)), sets
the value of the argument variable to be the noun phrase meaning (e.g., X=john),
then sets the resulting sentence meaning to be the expression, which now has its
argument set (e.g., jumps(john)).

This all generalizes quite nicely to the more complex example, "John loves
Mary". Figure 5.8 illustrates what this looks like in Prolog. Note that the semantics
for loves has two arguments, and both of these are stuck on the front so they can
be got at.

This can be discussed more formally, without reference to Prolog, using the λ-
notation (pronounced lambda-notation). An expression like $\lambda x.jumps(x)$ is used

```
sentence(SMeaning) -->
    noun_phrase(NPMeaning), verb_phrase(VPMeaning),
    {combine(NPMeaning, VPMeaning, SMeaning)}.

verb_phrase(VPMeaning) -->
    verb(VMeaning), noun_phrase(NPMeaning),
    {combine(NPMeaning, VMeaning, VPMeaning)}.

verb_phrase(VPMeaning) --> verb(VPMeaning).

noun_phrase(NPMeaning) --> proper_noun(NPMeaning).

proper_noun(john) --> [john].
proper_noun(mary) --> [mary].
verb(X^jumps(X)) --> [jumps].
verb(Y^X^loves(X,Y)) --> [loves].
```

Figure 5.8 *A Simple Grammar with Semantics: Final Version.*

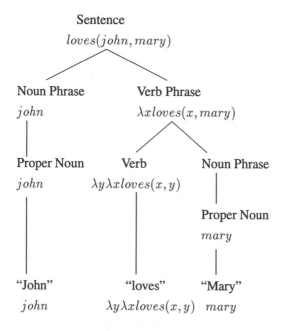

Figure 5.9 *Parse Tree with Associated Semantics.*

to represent an expression that when *applied* to an argument (say, $john$) results in that argument being substituted for X (i.e., to give $jumps(john)$). Applying $\lambda y.\lambda x.loves(x, y)$ to $mary$ gives $\lambda x.loves(x, mary)$. Applying this result to $john$ gives $loves(john, mary)$.

Figure 5.9 illustrates how this relates to the *structure* of the sentence obtained through parsing. The figure gives the parse tree for "John loves Mary" annotated with the meanings. Note that the meaning for the verb phrase is based simply on combining the meanings of its parts, while the meaning of the whole sentence is based simply on combining the verb phrase meaning and the noun phrase meaning. In the Prolog example the meanings are constructed at the same time as the sentence is parsed. However, it would also work to use the parse tree and the word meanings to find the sentence meaning after the parse is complete.

5.5 Pragmatics

From what we have discussed so far we can use speech recognition, syntactic and semantic analysis techniques to get from a speech signal of someone saying "John loves Mary" to an expression in predicate logic: $loves(john, mary)$. This uses knowledge of the sounds that make up words, of the structure of the language, and of the meanings of individual words. Yet to really understand language knowing the meanings of the individual words isn't enough. You need to know something about the *context* of the utterance: where it was said, by whom and why, and what was said before. This section will consider two aspects of this.

5.5.1 Language as Action

To appreciate why it isn't enough to stop after semantic analysis we can look first at the role language plays in *communication* and *action*. When we are talking to someone each utterance has a purpose. Sometimes that purpose is just to communicate some fact. So, if we say "John loves Mary" maybe the sole purpose of that utterance is to communicate this fact, and get the hearer to add the fact $loves(john, mary)$ to their "knowledge base", so to speak. However, often we have a deeper purpose, as illustrated in the following utterances:

1. "Where is the coffee?" The purpose here is obviously to find out where the coffee is. But the underlying goal may be to make some coffee.
2. "Can you close the window?" The purpose here is to get the hearer to shut the window. However, if taken as a literal statement, it just asks about the hearer's ability to perform this act.
3. "Do you have the time?" The purpose here is to find out the time. This is asked *indirectly* by asking the hearer if they know the time.
4. "When will you be home?" The purpose here perhaps depends on the speaker. Maybe it's the hearer's husband and the purpose is to check when he should put the dinner on. Maybe it's a friend wanting to find out a convenient time to call round.
5. "You're late." The immediate purpose is to tell the hearer that they are late. But the underlying purpose may be to criticize the hearer and make them feel bad.

Language is used here to achieve something. An utterance can be viewed as an *action* much as opening a door is an action. Indeed, utterance 2 above should (with luck) achieve much the same as the action of going to the window and shutting it yourself! The term *speech act* is used to refer to the actions that can be achieved through language. Types of speech act include *informing*, *requesting*, and *promising*. Behind each speech act there will be a goal – that is, something the speaker[6] wants to achieve.

We can try to express the goals that lie behind an utterance. If the speaker is denoted S and the hearer H then we might have the following goals:

1. S wants H to inform him where the coffee is.
2. S wants H to shut the window.

---

[6]Although we've talked about the speaker and the hearer, this also largely applies if there is a writer and reader. The writer is trying to achieve something through his or her text.

3. S wants H to tell him the time.

4. S wants H to tell him when she will be home.

5. S wants H to know that she is annoyed that he is late.

The hearer has to be able to recognize what these goals are in order to respond appropriately. It is not enough just knowing what an utterance literally means; we also need to know what the speaker's underlying message is.

This analysis of the goals behind an utterance is just one aspect of *pragmatics*. Ideas from *planning* (briefly discussed in Chapter 4) turn out to be important here. If language is used to achieve goals, just like other actions, then deciding what to say is a planning process. Working out the goals underlying a speaker's utterances, in order to respond appropriately, is a *plan recognition* problem. This is the opposite of planning. While in planning you start with a goal and find actions to achieve that goal, in plan recognition you start with the actions (in this case, utterances) and work out what the underlying goal was. Some knowledge of the context is useful when doing this analysis. For example, if the question "Do you know what time it is?" is asked in a situation where the hearer has arrived late to a meeting, then the utterance might be interpreted as a criticism, and the correct response is NOT "Yes". If it is uttered in a situation where the speaker needs to know the time then a correct response might be "Yes, it's 5 o'clock".

5.5.2 Handling Pronouns

A very different problem concerns the analysis of sentences which contain pronouns (i.e., words like "he", "she" and "it"). Consider the following utterance.

"Hamish kisses Shona. He loves her."

Clearly "he" refers to Hamish, while "her" refers to Shona. The interpretation of the second sentence should therefore be $loves(hamish, shona)$. But to obtain that interpretation it is clearly necessary to look at the previous sentence. Previous sentences provide the context in which later sentences are interpreted.

In the above case it was pretty clear who the pronouns referred to. "He" refers to the male entity mentioned in the previous sentence, while "she" refers to the female entity. It would be easy enough to write a program that handled this, using information about objects in the previous sentence to work out the meaning of the current sentence.

However, although this might work for many sentences it would not work for all. Sometimes a pronoun may refer to an entity mentioned several sentences back. Consider:

"John buys a new telescope. He sees Mary in the distance. He gets out his telescope. He looks at her through it."

The pronoun "her" in this example clearly refers to Mary, who was not mentioned at all in the previous sentence. Notice too in this example John's telescope is referred to in three ways: "a new telecope", "his telescope", and "it". Working out that the new telescope mentioned in the first sentence is the same as "his telescope" in the third sentence is not trivial. It really requires an understanding of what it means to buy something – that you then possess it.

This problem of finding out what things refer to isn't restricted to pronouns. Any noun phrase may refer to a particular object, and it may be important to work out which object that is to properly interpret the sentence. As an example, consider "John saw a blue Nissan Micra and a red Ford Fiesta in the garage. He decided to buy the blue car." The phrase "the blue car" clearly refers to the Nissan Micra.

Although most of the examples here have been rather artificial, this is an issue that has to be addressed in any practical natural language system. For example, in a airline database query system someone might well ask two questions such as "When is the next flight to Budapest?" followed by "Does it have any seats left?" It would be necessary to determine that "it" refers to a particular flight to Budapest, not Budapest itself.

5.6   Ambiguity in Language

One of the main problems in language understanding, which has only been vaguely alluded to up until now, is the problem of *ambiguity*. That is, most utterances have more than one possible interpretation. This section will summarize the kinds of ambiguity that occur, and how the right interpretation may be chosen.

Ambiguities occur at all stages of natural language understanding. The following list gives some of the ambiguities that occur at each stage.

Ambiguities in Speech Recognition: One problem here is that many quite different words sound just the same, for example "bear" and "bare" mentioned earlier. These are called *homophones*.

Syntactic ambiguity: Here there are two problems. First, a given word may have more than one possible syntactic category: "bat" can be a noun or a verb, for example. Second, a sentence may have more than one structure: "John saw Mary on the hill with a telescope" is an example of this discussed earlier. If the first kind of ambiguity occurs the second is more likely. In the sentence "Fruit flies like a banana" the word "flies" can be a noun or a verb. If it is interpreted as a verb then we get fruit flying across the room, in the same manner that a banana would fly across the room.

Semantic ambiguity: A new problem is introduced when we look at word meanings. Many words (even with the same syntactic category) may have more than one meaning. A much-used example is "bank" which can be a river bank or a financial institution. This is normally referred to as lexical ambiguity.

Spoken Natural Language Dialogue Systems

There are relatively few systems in existence that can engage in a spoken dialogue with the user, including interpreting their spoken utterances and generating a spoken response. One example system is the MIT PEGASUS system. The PEGASUS system is a spoken language interface to an airline reservation system, which allows people to obtain flight information and make flight reservations.

The system accepts spoken utterances and translates these into a representation of the meaning of the utterance. Contextual information is used where required. The system may have to prompt the user for further details or clarification until it can construct a complete database query.

The speech recognition component has a vocabulary of about 2,500 words and knows about 250 major cities worldwide. Although it has not yet been used in practice, the members of the research group who developed it have been able to use it to make actual travel arrangements.

Several other spoken language systems have been developed at MIT, including the older VOYAGER system which could answer questions about Massachusetts, such as how to get to a particular restaurant. This system could accept input in English, Italian or Japanese.

No spoken language dialogue system will correctly interpret every utterance, so the practical usability of these systems depends on how well they can recover from misinterpreting or failing to interpret something.

Pragmatic ambiguity: It is sometimes unclear which object a pronoun refers to. This is referred to as *referential ambiguity*. It also may be unclear what the speaker's goals are. Is the utterance "Do you know what time it is?" a criticism or a genuine question?

Sometimes, ambiguities that occur early in the understanding process may be resolved later on. For example, suppose the speech recognition system suggested that the word sequence could be one of:

"He read the book."
"He red the book."

The second alternative would have no valid parse according to a reasonable grammar of English, so could be rejected.

However, sometimes it is necessary to resort to general knowledge of the world, the speaker and/or the context in order to resolve ambiguities. For example, the odd interpretation of "Fruit flies like a banana" could be ruled out if we know that fruit tends not to fly. The correct version of "bank" in "Richard went to the bank to ask about a mortgage" could be chosen if we know that it is the financial version that deals with mortgages.

Clearly getting all this right requires quite a lot of general knowledge about the world. However fancy your natural language understanding system, it will fail to get the right interpretation of every utterance unless you also have a knowledge base including a large amount of everyday information.

5.7   Generation

There is more to being able to communicate in natural language than just being able to *understand* utterances. You have to be able to talk back too! That is, starting from some idea of what you want to communicate and some information that could be communicated, you need to be able to work out a sequence of words to express this. As an example, suppose the system in question is a database query system which can be used over the phone. The system might know that it has to tell the user about all the cheap flights from London to Boston on a given day, have the flight data available in its database, and have to come up with an utterance like the following:

> "There are two flights that might suit you. The first is with British Airways, costs £330, and leaves at 11am. The second is with American Airlines, costs £340, and leaves at 2pm. There are other flights available, but they are all more expensive."

Natural language generation can be broken up into stages, somewhat similar to those in natural language understanding. The first of these stages is deciding *what to say*. In the example above, given the goal to tell the user about cheap flights to Boston the system decides to mention the British Airways and American Airlines flights. The system must also decide how to organize this information, so that the passage reads sensibly. Here, the British Airways flight is mentioned first (maybe because it's cheaper?), and the utterance ends with an overview of other possible flights. Other orderings of the pieces of information may read less well.

Deciding what to say is sometimes referred to as *text planning*. The idea is to start with a goal and find a sequence of utterances that will achieve the goal. Planning techniques (as discussed in Chapter 4) are sometimes used for this, but it is also possible to use simpler techniques where standard ways for expressing things are encoded in some way. For our flight example, perhaps every flight query is answered by mentioning how many suitable flights there are, giving the cost and time of each one, and telling the user if there are other possible flights that are less suitable. If every flight query can be answered in this way there is no need to use complex techniques to plan what to say.

Having decided what to say a system must still determine *how to say it* – that is, the actual sequence of words to express the material. From some semantic representation such as, say, $cost(flight1, 330) \wedge leavetime(flight1, 1100) \wedge airline(flight1, ba)$, the system must decide that an appropriate utterance is "The first is with British Airways, costs £330, and leaves at 11am".

This can be a complex process. First it may be necessary to decide how to split up the information into separate sentences. For example, the information in the second and third sentences in the example could also be expressed as:

"There is a British Airways flight and an American Airline one, leaving at 11am and 2pm respectively. The flight with British Airways costs £330 and the one with American Airlines costs £340."

Having decided on the best way to split up the information, each sentence must be produced. The sentence should be grammatical, make appropriate use of pronouns, and use words that the hearer or reader is likely to understand. Getting all of this right is a complex problem. However, if there are only a few different basic kinds of sentences that will be required by a system it is possible to cheat by using some that you "prepared earlier", so to speak. For example, we could have a fill-in-the-blanks template such as "There is a flight with X which costs Y and leaves at Z".

The methods used by a natural language generation system depend on the flexibility required. If it is to be used with a special-purpose application system, where only a few different kinds of utterance are required, then we can cheat and use fill-in-the-blanks templates, handcrafted for the particular application. This is basically the same as the *mail-merge* systems used in word processors to produce personalized mailshots. If more flexibility is required then fancier methods are required, taking into account the issues discussed in this section.

Before leaving this section we should consider *speech synthesis*. If speech output is required we need a method to get from the words in a sentence to a suitable speech signal. If there are only a few possible basic sentence forms (perhaps produced with fill-in-the-blanks templates) then it is possible just to use recordings of a human saying the relevant phrases, and string the recordings of the required phrases together. This technology is used for train station announcements, for example. If more flexibility was required you could record someone saying every word in a dictionary. But this would be time consuming and take up a lot of memory.

A more sensible approach would seem to be to look up the phonetic spelling of each word, have recordings of each phoneme, and string together these. However, although this kind of works it results in rather poor and barely intelligible output. There are a number of problems. One is that phonemes are pronounced slightly differently according to what is said before and after them. Another is that the intonation, stress and timing used is important (e.g., rising in pitch near the end of a sentence when asking a question, pausing after an important point), and this cannot be determined from the words alone.

In spite of these problems there has been good progress in the development of speech synthesis systems, and it is possible to get quite intelligible output given some text to be spoken.

5.8 Summary

- Natural language processing involves both *understanding* where the meaning of an utterance is worked out given the sequence of words, and *generation*, where the sequence of words is worked out given something to be expressed.
- Natural language understanding can be divided into speech recognition, syntactic analysis, semantic analysis and pragmatics. Refer back to Figure 5.1 for an overview.
- Speech recognition involves finding the sequence of words given a speech signal. It involves matching fragments of the speech signal with known sounds (phonemes), and putting together possible phonemes to find possible words.
- Syntactic analysis involves using a *grammar* of the language to find the structure of the sentence.
- Semantic analysis involves using knowledge of the meanings of words and the structure of the sentence to find a representation of the meaning of the sentence.
- Pragmatics involves using *context* to fill out this meaning, for example finding out what objects the pronouns refer to.
- All these stages can have *ambiguous* output where more than one possible result is possible. For example, "bank" has two meanings. Sometimes world knowledge can be used to decide which is the right interpretation.
- Natural language generation can also be divided into stages. These are basically deciding what to say, deciding how to say it, and then (if speech output is required) working out the speech signal from the chosen words.

5.9 Further Reading

Most AI texts have one or more chapters on natural language processing, including (Rich & Knight, 1991) (ch.15), (Luger & Stubblefield, 1993) (ch.10), (Ginsberg, 1993) (ch.17) and (Russell & Norvig, 1995) (chs.22–24). Each talks about the main stages of analysis: syntax, semantics and pragmatics. Rich & Knight give a fairly broad coverage of different techniques, and contrasts with this chapter which presents one approach (DCGs and compositional semantics) in a consistent fashion. Ginsberg's approach is similar to that here, but he bases his examples on *augmented transition networks* rather than DCGs. Russell and Norvig give a fairly deep treatment, consistent with that presented here, but introducing further concepts and distinctions. For example, they talk about the use of *quasi-logical form* which contains both syntactic and semantic information.

There are many good textbooks devoted to natural language processing. A good basic book which develops the ideas in Sections 5.2 and 5.3 is (Pereira & Shieber, 1987). That book would follow on very naturally from this chapter, particularly for someone who wanted to implement a small, but non-trivial natural language understanding system in Prolog. Other more comprehensive texts that give overviews of the whole topic include (Allen, 1995) and (Gazdar & Mellish, 1989).

The above texts say little about speech processing, which tends to be treated as a separate topic. A good text on speech processing is (Holmes, 1988).

5.10 Exercises

The following is a grammar of a subset of English in DCG notation:

```
sentence --> np(N), vp(N).
np(N) --> det, noun(N).
vp(N) --> verb(N), np(_).

noun(s) --> [carrot].
noun(s) --> [rabbit].
noun(p) --> [rabbits].
verb(s) --> [eats].
det --> [the].
```

1. Which of the following sentences can be recognized with this grammar?

   - The carrot eats the carrot.

   - The rabbits eats the carrot.

   - The rabbit eats carrots.

2. Extend the grammar to handle sentences like the following. "All" and "some" should be treated as kinds of determiner (det).

   - All rabbits eat carrots.

   - Some rabbits eat the carrot.

   - The rabbit eats every carrot.

   The grammar should NOT allow sentences that are grammatically incorrect because a plural noun (e.g., carrots) is used with a determiner that can only be used with singular nouns (e.g., a, every) or vice versa, e.g.,

- All rabbit eat the carrot.

- A rabbits eat the carrot.

- Every rabbits eat the carrots.

Try out your grammar using Prolog.

3. Try giving the meaning of the first three sentences above using predicate logic, noting any difficulties you have in capturing the meaning of the English.

4. Suggest how you might extend the grammar if you wanted to rule out silly sentences (i.e., that are semantically odd). For example, you might want to eliminate sentences involving carrots eating rabbits. One approach would be to use extra arguments, and to assign nouns semantic categories such as "animate" or "eatable". Try to make your solution as general as possible.

CHAPTER 6

Vision

Aims:	To introduce the basics of computational vision, focusing on low-level processing.
Objectives:	You should be able to:
	Briefly describe the main stages of processing in vision.
	Explain how edges and lines may be found in an image.
	Outline the different methods for obtaining information about the depth and orientation of objects in an image.
	Discuss the problem of recognising objects.
Prerequisites:	Some basic mathematics, such as elementary calculus and trigonometry would be helpful.

6.1 Introduction

Following on from the previous chapter, we'll look at another "mundane" task: vision. People can easily make sense of what they see around them, easily recognizing complex objects – it is something we learn when we are very young. However, like natural language understanding, this is extremely hard to automate. A single object may be viewed from many different angles, in different lighting conditions, and possibly with other objects obscuring part of the view. So, just as with speech recognition, there is no simple mapping from a visual signal to a recognized object.

We'll assume that the purpose of a vision system is to get from an initial *digitized image* to some useful analysis of the scene. For some practical applications a very simple analysis may be useful. For example, in a system to sort objects on a conveyor belt into widgets and wodgets it may be quite easy to determine, from a simple silhouette image, which type of object it is. And a very simple robot vision system might just need to know when it is about to bump into something and which way to turn.

However, although many practical vision systems may have more modest requirements, an ultimate goal must be to develop a system with capabilities comparable to human capabilities. Consider the task of assembling some MFI kitchen units. We *recognize* the various parts (e.g., door, handle, etc.), *read* the instructions (well, interpret the weird diagrams), *navigate* round the various objects now scattered around the kitchen floor and *manipulate* the objects to assemble them. We have to get from the visual signal (from our eyes) to a representation of the scene which is adequate for carrying out complex operations on the relevant objects. This requires some knowledge of the specific objects (e.g., typical dimensions of kitchen cupboards), general knowledge about types of material (e.g., metal is shiny and smooth), and knowledge of how the light source, orientation of the object and type of material combine to affect the brightness at a given point in the image.

Like natural language processing, the vision process is normally divided up into stages. We start from a digitized image, which gives the brightness at each point (*pixel*) in the image. After this the stages are:

Low-level Processing: Here simple features are identified, such as lines or *edges* in the image. The output will be something like a line drawing of the objects in the image, the lines separating the image into regions corresponding to object surfaces. The term *primal sketch* is often used for this.

Medium-level Processing: The next stage is to work out how far away the regions are and what their orientation is. The output is sometimes referred to as the $2\frac{1}{2}$-D sketch.

High-level Processing: Finally we try to obtain a useful high level description of the scene. A first stage may be to work out 3-D models of objects in the scene given the depth and orientation information above. Next, one thing that might be done is to try to *recognize* what sorts of objects occur in the scene.

These stages are summarized in Figure 6.1. The rest of this chapter will look at each of these stages in more detail.

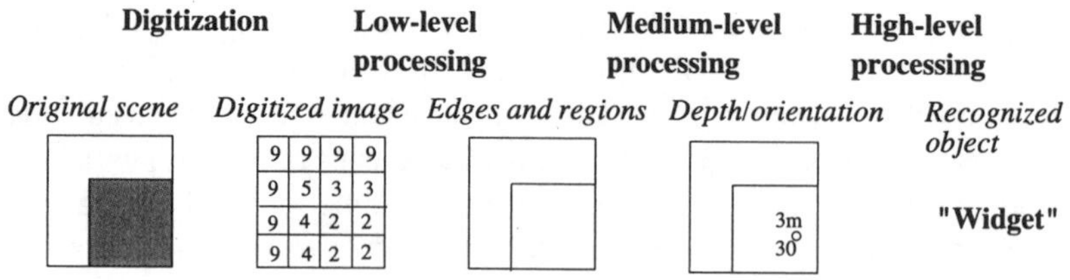

Figure 6.1 *Stages of Visual Processing.*

6.2 Low-level Processing

The first stage, then, is to extract some primitive features from the digitized image. Before discussing how this is done we should say something about the format of this image.

At its simplest a digitized image can be just a two-dimensional array indicating for each point in the image just how light or dark the picture is at this point. Figure 6.1 illustrates this for a tiny 4×4 image segment. However, a realistic image might require an array of around 512×512 to give a reasonably fine (*high resolution*) representation of the original image, and our 4×4 segment would just correspond to a very small square portion of an image. Each image point is referred to as a *pixel*, and the brightness or *image intensity* at a pixel is usually represented by an integer between 0 and 255 (0 = black, 255 = white).

A colour image can be represented in a similar manner but three arrays could be used for the amount of blue, green and red at different points in the image. However, to keep things simple we'll stick to black and white or *grey level* images.

Before the digitized image is processed further it may be necessary to remove *noise* and very fine detail from the image. Noise is just incorrect intensity values introduced in the process of producing the digitized image. Fine detail might be, say, the texture of the wall and carpet in a picture of my office. Removing this detail might allow the vision system to focus on the basic objects in the room without being distracted. This noise and fine detail is removed by *smoothing* the image. This basically involves replacing the intensity value at a given point with an average of the intensity values of this and surrounding points. The effect is to very slightly blur the image.

6.2.1 Edge Detection

Now we are ready to try to find simple features in the image. Our goal is to try to obtain something like a line drawing of the objects in the image, and the first stage of this is to find points that might lie on the edges of objects in the image.

To illustrate the process we will consider the image in Figure 6.2. The grid on the left illustrates a (much-simplified) array of intensity values (i.e., digitized image) for the simple picture on the right. To keep things simple the intensity values used are just 0–9 (0 = black; 9 = white). We'll assume we have an array I holding the image intensity values, so, for example, $I[2, 6] = 3$.

Note that, although the edges of the object in the original image are sharp, the intensity values at the pixels corresponding to those edges may fall part-way between the intensity of the background (9) and that of the main body of the object. That is because such a pixel falls part-way between the object and the background.

Nevertheless, it should be clear that the edges of the object (let's call it a house) can be found by looking for places where the intensity at nearby pixels is significantly different. For example, the lower half of the left-hand column of pixels all

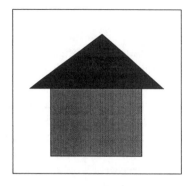

9	9	9	9	9	9	9	9	*0*
9	9	9	3	4	9	9	9	*1*
9	5	0	0	0	0	6	9	*2*
3	2	1	1	1	1	2	9	*3*
9	4	3	3	3	3	3	4	*4*
9	4	3	3	3	3	6	9	*5*
9	4	3	3	3	3	6	9	*6*
9	8	7	7	7	7	8	9	*7*

0   1   2   3   4   5   6   7

Figure 6.2 *Image Intensity Values for Simple Image.*

have intensity 9. The pixels in the next column on have lower values. This corresponds to the left-hand wall of the house. The bottom of the house isn't quite so clearly delimited, as the bottom row of pixels correspond partly to the house, partly to the background. However, there is still a fairly noticeable difference between those in the bottom row and those in the row above.

Differences between intensity values can be measured in the x-direction or the y-direction. For example, we could measure $I(x+1,y) - I(x,y)$ for different values of x and y, or we could measure $I(x,y+1) - I(x,y)$. The former would find vertical edges and the latter horizontal edges. For example, for $x = 0, y = 5$ we have $I(x+1,y) - I(x,y) = -5$. This is quite a big difference as there is a vertical edge.

From the discussion so far we could write a very simple program that could work out the differences in x- and y-directions for each point in the image, and mark in an edge if either of these differences exceeded some *threshold* (e.g., if the magnitude of the difference was greater than 2). The results could be written to a new array, with a 1 wherever there should be an edge and a 0 otherwise. Figure 6.3 illustrates the result for the example image if the threshold was 2. Although this very simple method has found some of the relevant edges in the image, it has missed some (the edge between the roof and the main part of the house), found some twice, and managed only a vague approximation to the angle of the roof.

One way to improve on this basic technique is to use slightly more complex difference operations. *Difference operators* can be represented as small masks (2×2 or 3×3 arrays) that are placed over groups of points in the image. The difference operation now involves taking each mask value, multiplying it by the corresponding image intensity value, and summing the results.

0	0	1	1	1	0	0
1	1	1	1	1	1	1
0	1	0	0	0	0	1
1	0	0	0	0	1	1
1	0	0	0	0	1	1
1	0	0	0	0	1	1
0	1	1	1	1	1	0

Figure 6.3 *Edges Detected in Example Image.*

For example, if we have a mask as follows:

```
-1   1
-1   1
```

and align it with $I[2..3, 1..2]$ then the relevant calculation is $2 \times 1 + 6 \times 1 - 1 \times 1 - 5 \times 1 = 2$. Again, we conclude that there is an edge if the magnitude of the resulting number is greater than some threshold.

This can be expressed more formally as follows. For a mask $M[x, y]$ (with centre of mask $M[0, 0]$) and image $I[x, y]$ we calculate:

$$I'[x, y] = \sum_i \sum_j I[x - i, y - j] \times M[i, j]$$

The above calculation is the discrete *convolution* of the image with the mask. If the result is above the threshold there is an edge point.

A variety of difference operators have been proposed. Some effectively combine finding differences with smoothing the image. One example is the *Sobel operator*, given below:

```
-1   0   1          1   2   1
-2   0   2          0   0   0
-1   0   1         -1  -2  -1
```

There are two versions, to find the difference in the x- and y-directions. By focusing on a 3×3 group of pixels a more reliable result can be obtained, avoiding spurious effects due to pixels right on the edge of an object in the image.

These difference operators give an idea of how fast the intensity is changing in a small region of the image. Where it is changing fast this means there is some interesting feature in the image, like the edge of an object (or a surface marking). The two operators above give the change in the x- and y-directions separately. If a single value is required giving the overall magnitude we can find the x and y

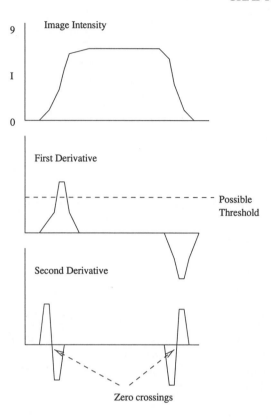

Figure 6.4 *Plots of Image Intensity and First and Second Spatial Derivatives.*

values (say, g_1 and g_2) and calculate $\sqrt{g_1^2 + g_2^2}$. We can also get an estimate of the direction of the edge: $\tan^{-1} \frac{g_1}{g_2}$.

This can all be described in terms of differentiation. What we're looking for are places where the rate of intensity change is high. This corresponds to the *spatial derivative* $\partial I / \partial x$ for the x-direction, and $\partial I / \partial y$ for the y-direction. The points most likely to correspond to an edge are in fact where this rate of intensity change is a maximum. Now, the first derivative $\partial I / \partial x$ is a maximum when the *second* derivative $\partial^2 I / \partial x^2 = 0$. So looking for edges corresponds to looking for where the second derivative is zero. As it may never be precisely zero we look for *zero crossings* where it crosses between a positive and a negative value. This is illustrated in Figure 6.4, which gives graphs for the intensity values across a horizontal cross-section of the example image, and for (discrete approximations to) the first and second derivatives[1].

A mask can be constructed based on the second derivative. This has the advan-

---

[1]The observant will note that the second derivative will also be zero when the first derivative is a *minimum*. These will not correspond to edges and will have to be filtered out.

tage over the previously discussed masks that it is not so sensitive to the *thresholds* chosen. This is also illustrated in Figure 6.4. If such a mask is combined with a particular (gaussian) *smoothing* operator then we get the Marr–Hildreth operator (discussed further in some of the references at the end of the chapter).

Although the operation required at each point in the image for these methods is very simple, edge detection is still a computationally expensive operation simply because of the large amount of data involved. For a 1024×1024 image the operation must be repeated over a million times. It can be made more efficient by detecting edges in different pixels in parallel. Figure 6.5 illustrates the output of an edge detection system for a picture of a robot arm.

6.2.2 Line Fitting: The Hough Transform

The output of the stage described above is just a set of points which are believed to lie on an intensity edge (Figure 6.3). It would be much more useful if these could be aggregated into lines corresponding to the boundaries of the objects. So, our "house" image could then just be represented as six lines corresponding to the edges of the front wall and the roof.

One way to try to find such lines might be to start with an edge point and then track along looking for other connected edge points. However, this does not work well if there are breaks in the line. For example, if there was a tree in front of the house then the edge of the roof might be broken up into two or more sections, as illustrated in Figure 6.6. It is also not clear how the lines so found should be represented. It would be easy enough to represent straight edges simply by their end points, but what about curved segments?

A solution to these problems is to use the *Hough transform*. The idea here

 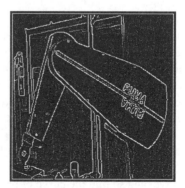

Figure 6.5 *Output of Edge Detection System.*

Figure 6.6 *House Obscured by Tree.*

is to consider the equations of the line (or curve) segments that you are trying to find. If we are just dealing with straight lines we know that all such lines can be represented by an equation of the form $y = mx + c$. If we have a point (x_1, y_1) that we know must lie on such a straight edge then we can check whether that point falls on a given line (i.e., whether for a particular value of m and c it is true that $y_1 = mx_1 + c$. Now, if we consider all possible straight lines (i.e., all values of m and c)[2], we can check for each line just how many points could be falling on it. We then find which lines have most points which could be on that line. We assume that these are the actual lines in the image.

This can be expressed more formally as follows. Suppose $edge(x, y)$ is a function that returns 1 if there is an edge point at (x, y), 0 otherwise. The Hough transform $h(m, c)$ is:

$$h(m, c) = \sum_{(x,y):mx+y=c} edge(x, y) \tag{6.1}$$

The lines we are after correspond to values for m and c which give a maximum value for $h(m, c)$.

Note that this method will treat the two parts of the roof in Figure 6.4 as part of the same line. The next problem is to check back with the image to find the end points of the line segments. However, this is easier now the equations of the lines have been found.

The nice thing about the Hough transform is that it also works just fine if the lines we are after are curve segments, such as arcs of a circle or even more complex curves. If, for example, we knew that the curves we were looking for could be approximated using a cubic expression of the form $y = ax^3 + bx^2 + cx + d$ then again we could find for each combination of a, b, c and d just how many points lay on that curve, and so find the curve of best fit.

Anyway, at the end of this process, whereas before we just had an array of edge

---

[2]Obviously as m and c take continuous values we can't explicitly consider them all, but can consider values between two points going up in small steps.

points, we now have some line or curve segments. These may well correspond to the boundaries between different objects.

Once the line segments have been obtained we need to work out how this splits up the image into *regions* corresponding to different surfaces. One approach is to look for regions of similar brightness. For example, the tree in Figure 6.6 could be identified as a separate region, as it is uniformly darker than the other areas in the scene. In fact, for simple applications edge detection and line fitting might be unnecessary, and we could just immediately look for such homogeneous regions.

If we want to find the boundaries between objects rather than surfaces (e.g., between the house and the tree, but not between the wall and the roof), one approach is to look carefully at the *junctions* where lines meet. For example, a T junction generally means that there is one object in front of another[3]. The *Waltz algorithm* develops this idea for simple images of blocks. Although it is not generally used in practical vision systems it is a neat technique that is discussed further in most of the references at the end of the chapter.

6.3 Obtaining Depth and Orientation Information

Now that regions (or at least lines) in the image have been identified we need to try to work out how far the objects are away from the viewer and what orientation the various surfaces are at. For example, in our house image, is this a two-inch high toy house a few inches away from the camera, or is it a full-sized house in the distance?

There are a variety of different techniques and sources of information that can be used to determine this. We can look at the *shading* and *texture* of the objects to get clues about orientation. To work out distance information we can see how the view of the object changes as you move past it, or obtain images from two eyes or nearby cameras and use differences between the two images. These different techniques are briefly discussed below.

6.3.1 Stereo Vision

Humans make use of both eyes when guessing how far away objects are. People with poor sight in one eye tend to be worse at estimating distance (if there aren't common-sense clues to help them). If you close one eye you may find that your sense of distance is less good.

Stereo vision uses the fact that, if the object you are looking at is very close, it will appear in a different position in the images from each eye. If the object is a long way away then it will look the same in both eyes. Try looking at a pencil held up in front of you, closing each eye in turn. You should find that when the pencil is

---

[3]In the example figure this would actually suggest that the roof was a separate object. This is because the roof tilts down in front of the house.

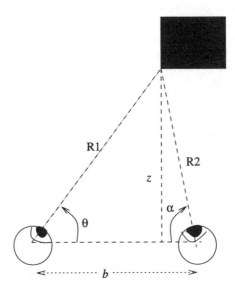

Figure 6.7 *Stereo Vision.*

held close to your nose it "moves" in the field of vision when you switch from one eye to the other. If the pencil is held at arm's length (or preferably further) then it stays pretty much in one place.

The distance of the object from the viewer can be found using simple trigonometry if we know the angle of that object from each eye (or camera). Those angles can be obtained by looking at the position of the object in each image.

Consider Figure 6.7, where someone is looking at the corner of a box. If we know the angles α and θ, and the spacing between the eyes (b), then with a little elementary geometry we can find out how far the box is away from the viewer. We can use the sine law, to conclude that:

$$\frac{R1}{\sin \alpha} = \frac{b}{\sin (180^\circ - \theta - \alpha)}$$

Now, as $z = R1 \sin \theta$, we can conclude that:

$$z = \frac{b \sin \alpha sin\theta}{\sin (180^\circ - \theta - \alpha)}$$

So, from knowing the directions in which an image point is perceived in each eye we can work out how far that image point is away.

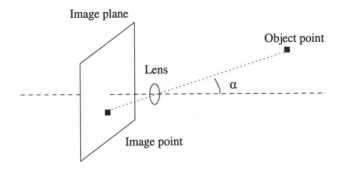

Figure 6.8 *Projection of Object on Image Plane.*

The angles θ and α can be determined quite straightforwardly from the position that the object appears in the image. Figure 6.8 illustrates the relationship between the angle and the position in the image.

Now, this is all very well, but there is one tricky problem. How do we know that a particular image point in one eye corresponds to another particular image point in another? Or to put it another way, how do we find the correspondences between the two images? This is vital for stereopsis, as the whole process relies on using the viewing angles from each eye to a common point in space.

So, the hard bit of stereopsis is developing good algorithms for doing this feature matching. This may be difficult. For example, consider the scene in Figure 6.6. Perhaps the top of the tree in one image (say, from the right-hand camera) is in almost the same position as the top of the house in the other image. As they look kind of similar the two might be confused. Finding correspondences involves not just looking for similar features, but exploiting geometric properties of the two images and likely properties of the physical scene (e.g., distances don't change rapidly from pixel to pixel except at edges of objects).

6.3.2 Depth from Motion

A closely related method for finding distance information is to use successive images from a moving camera. To see roughly how this works consider Figure 6.9.

Here we have John, out for a walk up the road to Mary's house. That's the one with the tree. He first looks up and sees Mary's house up in front. A minute later he looks up and the house is kind of to the side. If he absent-mindedly walks past her house then a minute later he has to look back to see the house. The viewing angle to the house is constantly changing as he walks along.

On the other hand, more distant objects like the mountains in the distance and the sun in the sky always appear in about the same place.

This might look like it would just involve exactly the same techniques as stereo vision. However, we may not know precisely where the camera is at each point.

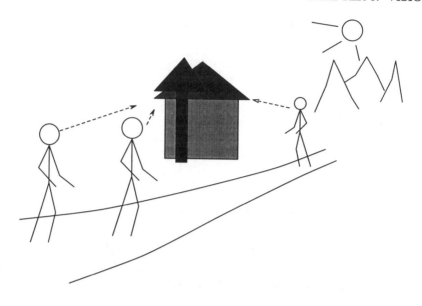

Figure 6.9 *Change of Viewing Angle with Motion.*

So on the one hand we may have less accurate information about camera position, but on the other hand we can get *lots* of images by taking a picture repeatedly as we move along. It turns out that we can work out the direction and motion of the observer by looking at how different parts of the image appear to move between successive frames. This can then be used in working out the shape of the objects in the scene.

6.3.3   Texture and Shading

Texture and shading can be used to obtain clues about the orientation of objects in the scene. The use of texture is illustrated in Figure 6.10. By texture we just mean regularly repeated patterning. The change in shape of the repeated patterning on the floor suggests a surface receding into the distance. The changing patterning on the cube reinforces our perception of its (cuboid) shape.

Figure 6.11 illustrates how information may be obtained from shading. The shape of the details of my ceiling cornice can be determined (largely) from the change in shading (or brightness) in the image. Similarly, the curves in my sofa can be partially determined by the change in shading. There are algorithms for determining shape given such shading information, but they rely on there being a simple uniform light source and objects with fairly regular colour and *reflectance* (shininess).

Figure 6.10 *Determining Orientation from Texture.*

Figure 6.11 *Determining Orientation from Shading.*

6.4 Object Recognition

From the analysis so far we have, in principle, partitioned the image into regions and determined the depth (distance from the viewer) and orientation of these regions. These regions should correspond to surfaces of the objects. Now the goal is to recognize the objects in the scene.

This is clearly only possible if the system knows about the objects that might appear in the scene. If there is a carrot in the scene, but there is no knowledge in the system about what carrots look like, then the system has no chance of guessing that the knobbly orange stick thing is a carrot. So practically, object recognition is restricted to where there is a relatively small number of objects that might occur in the scene, and the system has information about all these objects.

For example, suppose we have a set of wooden toys, including a house, a church, a tree, and a family of four toy people. These are to be arranged on a nice uniform green mat to form a scene. It should be possible to analyse a picture of this scene, recognizing each object in the scene, determining its position, and perhaps even coming up with a formal description of the arrangement (e.g., `nextto(tree, church)`). This is obviously much easier than the task of recognizing the diverse objects that might occur in a real village scene. Not only are there a very large number of possible objects that might appear in the real scene, but a particular type of object might come in many shapes and sizes! There is no one standard appearance for a tree, a person or even a house.

To keep things simple we'll assume that the scene we are to analyse is based on such a set of wooden toys. The image might be similar to that which we've been considering to date (Figure 6.6), but with more objects in the scene and a more three-dimensional view of the objects. Although this is obviously still an artificial problem, it is comparable to some practical problems where a robot is manipulating some engineered objects.

Even this simplified problem is far from trivial. Each object can be viewed from a number of different angles, looking quite different from each perspective. An object can also be near or far from the camera, appearing large or small in the image. And, just to add a touch of realism, we will assume that the toy people have movable arms and legs, which can be in different positions.

Now, one way to do object recognition is as follows. To recognize an object we need a *model* of that object. Recognition will involve trying to find good matches between the scene and the model. Now, if we are dealing with three-dimensional objects, which look different from different angles, we need three-dimensional models. Such models can be composed from *volumetric primitives* like cones, spheres, blocks and cylinders. Figure 6.12 gives a possible model based on these primitives for our toy man.

Matching can now proceed in two stages. In the first the surfaces in the scene are matched to possible volumetric primitives. The output of this stage would be a description of the scene in terms of these primitives (e.g., a cylinder of dimensions D at angle A in position P). Having described the scene in this way these primitives can then be matched against the object models. For example, if the first stage had identified a sphere above a large cylinder with four smaller cylinders to the side and below, then this might be successfully matched with the toy man model and the object identified.

Now, for our simplified wooden toy problem this matching with the models may be relatively simple. The only complications might arise due to the varied positions of the arms and legs, and the similarities between the different toy people (toy man versus toy woman versus toy child). We can consider how the approach would extend to more realistic scenes. Obviously more models would be required, and the models would have to be better, for example capturing the allowable variability between, say, different trees. The models might also need to be more detailed. However, for detailed models we need an efficient way to match them. It may then be necessary to match in several stages, first considering coarse features, then finer ones.

However, even this would probably not be enough. When humans recognize objects in a complex scene we use general knowledge of where different objects are expected to be (e.g., humans don't normally fly across the sky, unless it's Super-

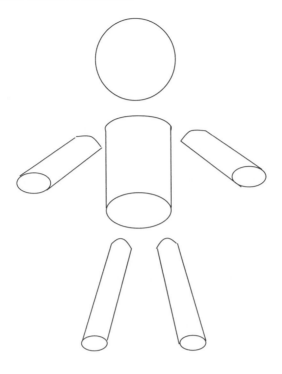

Figure 6.12 *A Simple Object Model for a Toy Man.*

man), and what these objects may be doing (children don't normally drive cars, so that's probably an adult). Properly understanding a visual scene is very *knowledge intensive*.

There are many analogies we can draw here with natural language understanding, particularly speech recognition. Just as an object may take many forms and be perceived in different ways, words may be pronounced in many ways and in different contexts. So recognizing words and recognizing objects from the speech or visual signal is a complex task. Both tasks involve some matching process, but this is not straightforward, as the models for words or objects will be complex and must capture wide variability.

6.5   Practical Vision Systems

So far we've assumed that the goal of the vision system is to recognize objects in a scene, given one or more images of that scene. A particular process has been outlined, which may be used successfully for simple scenes involving a small collection of block-like objects.

Practical Applications

One of the most common applications of vision systems is in manufacturing, and in particular for assembly line tasks. The task of the vision
system may be for quality control (recognizing defective parts) or to
identify and localize (i.e., determine the position of) objects on the assembly line ready for a robotic arm to take some appropriate action.
Everything happens on a planar surface, objects may be moved (along
the conveyor belt) into optimal positions, lighting is controlled, and
there is a uniform colour background against which objects are recognized. This significantly simplifies the vision problem, and relatively
simple methods may be used. For example, edge detection methods
may be unnecessary, and instead the whole image may be *thesholded*
to separate the objects from the background.

However, the problems involved are still not trivial. The objects may
be very complex, appear in various orientations, be overlapping, and
be shiny (causing reflection effects). Both recognizing and finding the
precise position of such objects is still a challenging problem.

For different applications different approaches may be required. For example,
a practical recognition system might be able to set things up so that the objects in
question are always in exactly the same orientation. (They may be forced physi-
cally into a corner, for example, or might be engineered so that there is a marking
indicating orientation.) If this is the case simpler recognition methods may be adequate, perhaps using the array of edge points rather than attempting to determine
regions, distances and volumes.

Practical vision systems are also not restricted to using methods similar to
those humans use. For example, rather than use conventional camera images, it
is possible to use *sonar* to determine the distance of the objects from the viewer.
Here a signal is bounced off the object and the time taken for it to come back to a
detector used to estimate distance.

It is also not necessary to have a passive observer. A particularly important
development in vision is the idea of *active vision*. When we as humans try to make
sense of a strange object we may move our heads and walk around the object to get
a better view. If an interesting object is seen we focus on that object so that object
is centred in our field of vision. It turns out that computer vision is also easier
if we have a movable camera which can be controlled as required by the visual
processing.

Finally we should note that object recognition isn't the only goal of computer vision. At the beginning of this chapter we considered a scenario involving

recognizing, *manipulating* and *navigating around* some objects. Navigation is a particularly important task, with the development of *autonomous vehicles* which are meant to travel, driverless, into dangerous and rough terrain. For this task it may not matter whether each object in the scene is recognized, but it does matter that the vehicle tends to keep to any roads and avoids bumping into large obstacles. The methods used for this task are rather different to those discussed above. However, finding distances and *structure* from successive images received as the vehicle is in motion turns out to be particularly useful.

6.6 Summary

- Computer vision involves interpreting a scene given a digital image giving the intensity values at different points.

- The analysis is normally divided into stages. In low-level processing simple features like edges are detected and the image partitioned into regions corresponding to surfaces. In medium-level processing depth and orientation information is found using a variety of methods. Finally in high-level processing a useful representation of the scene is obtained, perhaps recognizing objects by matching models of possible objects with the surface found in the image.

- Practical vision systems may make use of the fact that the objects to be recognized can be manipulated or the camera moved.

6.7 Further Reading

Although many longer AI texts have material on vision it is not always presented well. There is a good short chapter in (Ginsberg, 1993), while (Russell & Norvig, 1995) (ch.24) contains some more technical material, but it is less clear than their usual. A good but rather mathematical treatment is given in (Dean, 1995).

A classic text on vision is (Marr, 1982). This clearly presents a particular theory focusing on a computational theory of human visual processing. It is perhaps particularly useful for its material on edge detection. A good general textbook on vision is (Ballard & Brown, 1982). Although an old text, it is still probably a good place to start. Two more up-to-date texts, with pointers to the more recent literature, are (Nalwa, 1993) and (Jain, 1995).

6.8 Exercises

1. Sketch the graph of intensity against x for the image in Figure 6.2, $y = 6$. Sketch too the first and second derivative, and show that the edges correspond to zero crossings in the second derivative.

2. Use the Sobel operator from Section 6.2.1 to find the edge points in the image in Figure 6.2. Assume a threshold of 3.

3. The Hough transform involves finding how many edge points fit each of the various possible lines. Try finding the diagonal lines of the left-hand side of the roof, given your result from question 2, by counting how many edge points fit the line $y = x + c$ for $c = 0..5$.

4. Suppose we are looking for *circles* in the image. The equation of a circle is $ax^2 + by^2 = c$. Outline how the Hough transform would be used to find possible circles.

5. Give two reasons why it may be useful to move the camera in order to identify objects in the image.

6. (Project) Implement a simple edge detection program based on the Sobel operator. You should decide on the image format that your program will handle. One simple choice would be the grey-scale version of the portable bitmap (pbm) format.

CHAPTER 7

Machine Learning and Neural Networks

Aims:	To introduce the basics of machine learning, particularly inductive learning, focusing on *version space search*, *decision tree induction*, *neural networks* and *genetic algorithms*.
Objectives:	You should be able to:
	Describe how each method can be used to perform *classification* tasks – given some input features you should be able to describe how the output classification is determined.
	Compare and contrast the different methods, commenting on the suitability for different kinds of problems.
Prerequisites:	Chapters 2 and 4.

7.1 Introduction

The ability to learn is arguably one of the most crucial characteristics of an intelligent entity. A system that can learn is both more flexible, being able to respond to new problems and situations, and may also be easier to program. The first point should be self-evident. The second is becoming increasingly important in expert systems development – if experts cannot clearly articulate how they can solve problems then maybe they can be given some example problems to solve, and a learning program used to obtain some general rules from these example cases.

Learning is still an expanding area of AI research. It overlaps with almost all other areas of AI: in planning and robotics, there is interest in getting systems to learn rules of behaviour from experience in some environment; in natural language a system may learn syntactic rules from example sentences; in vision a system may learn to recognize some object given some example images; and in expert systems rules may be learned from example cases. It is also an area which is attracting interest in industry, with many commercial products available. For example, there is interest in analysing data obtained from supermarket loyalty cards in order to find rules that can be used in direct marketing campaigns.

There are several different basic kinds of learning, involving different amounts of effort on the part of learner and teacher. A teacher may tell you something directly, so you just have to remember it; they may give some examples ("Fido and Rover are both dogs."); present an analogy ("Electricity in wires is like water in pipes."); or you may have to discover new knowledge for yourself, through experimentation and introspection.

In AI most of the work to date has been on learning from examples, or *inductive learning*. This may involve learning conceptual categories (like the concept of "dog", from examples of dogs), learning rules to predict the weather, learning rules to diagnose a disease, and so on. In each case examples are given in some suitable formalism, and the system attempts to infer general rules or descriptions from those examples. The examples may be positive (Fido's a dog) or negative (Herbert's not).

In general, inductive learning is used to train a system to perform *classification tasks*. We can think of a classification task as any problem where there are a number of *input features* that influence the answer, and an enumerable set of possible *output categories*. For example, medical diagnosis is a classification task, where the input features are the patient's symptoms, and the output categories are the possible diagnoses. Character recognition (e.g., recognizing that a scanned-in character is the letter "p") is another kind of classification task – here the input features may be features of the character analysed (e.g., it has a long straight bit down the left side), and the output category is the recognized character. If a problem can be expressed in terms of a fixed set of input features and a smallish number of possible output categories, and there are examples available (e.g., people who have been diagnosed by experts; characters identified by humans), then inductive learning methods may be used to try to produce a system to automatically produce the correct classification given just the input feature values.

This chapter introduces a number of contrasting techniques for inductive learning, starting with *symbolic* methods, where the learned concept is represented using the sorts of knowledge representation languages introduced in Chapter 2. Two main approaches will be discussed. In the first method, learning is seen as a search problem, and the methods allow the *search space* of possible concepts to be searched to find one that matches the examples. The second approach involves building up the best *decision tree* (a simple flow-chart-like representation) to categorize the given examples.

Next, the use of *genetic algorithms* in inductive learning will be introduced. Genetic algorithms are based on the notion that good solutions or designs can *evolve* out of a population, by combining possible solutions to produce "offspring" solutions and "killing off" the weaker of those solutions.

Finally we will discuss learning in neural networks. Neural networks, loosely based on the architecture of the brain, have been widely discussed in the press, and are a promising approach for certain tasks. They are discussed in this chapter next to the more "traditional" AI approaches such as decision tree induction so as to highlight the similarities and differences. However, both genetic algorithms and neural networks are important topics in their own right, with applications beyond those discussed here (and indeed, not limited to machine learning).

In order to best compare and contrast the methods a simple example will be used throughout. This will be introduced in the next section.

7.2   A Simple Inductive Learning Example

Real machine learning applications typically require many hundreds or even thousands of examples in order for interesting knowledge to be learned. For example, to learn rules to diagnose a particular disease, given that the patient has, say, stomach pains, data on thousands of patients would be required, listing the additional symptoms of each patient and the final diagnoses made by an expert.

However, to illustrate the methods a simpler problem and set of examples are required. For the rest of this chapter the main problem that will be discussed is the following, which we'll refer to later as the "student" problem.

Suppose we have data on a number of students in last year's class, and are trying to find a rule that will allow us to determine whether current students are likely to get a first-class degree mark. We will assume the data that we have on last year's students includes: whether they got the equivalent of a first class mark last year; whether they work hard; male or female; and whether they go out drinking a lot. For each we also know whether they did in fact get a first. The ones that did are referred to as *positive examples* while the ones who didn't are referred to as *negative examples*. Six such students are to be considered, illustrated in Figure 7.1.

A quick inspection should show that the two people who got firsts (Alan and Gail) both got firsts last year and work hard, and that none of the people who failed to get firsts both did well last year and work hard. So a reasonable learned rule is that if you did well last year and work hard this year you should do OK. However,

Student	First last year?	Male?	Works hard?	Drinks?	First this year?
Richard	yes	yes	no	yes	no
Alan	yes	yes	yes	no	yes
Alison	no	no	yes	no	no
Jeff	no	yes	no	yes	no
Gail	yes	no	yes	yes	yes
Simon	no	yes	yes	yes	no

Figure 7.1 *Student Exam Performance Data.*

from the example data other rules are possible. For example, maybe the rule is that if you EITHER are male and don't drink OR are female and drink a lot then you'll do well. This rule does in fact cover the facts given, but is a little odd, and more complex than the other rule.

These two rules give different predictions for current students. Perhaps Robert got a first last year, works hard, but goes out drinking. By the first rule he should be OK, but by the second he'll fail to get a first (unless he gives up drinking). With such critical decisions to make it is clear that we need the best predictive rule to guide current behaviour. Generally the best rule, getting most predictions right, will be the simplest one, as it tends to capture generalities (hard-working students do well) rather than the idiosyncrasies of the specific students (Alan doesn't drink).

In this example we have selected four attributes (or *features*) to focus on: first last year, works hard, male/female and drinks. All these have yes/no answers. This is not, of course, the only way to present the examples. Perhaps other features are more important, such as what subjects they are studying, or what their mark is so far on coursework. It would also be possible to select features that don't have yes/no answers; "drinks a lot" could be changed to "drinking habits" with possible values excessive, moderate, occasional and never. These sorts of decisions, about what features to use for examples and what possible values these features can have, are extremely important in getting good performance out of a machine learning system.

However, for now we'll work with the above example, just to illustrate the methods. As there are four features, each with yes/no answers, there are 16 possible distinct types of student, and we have data on the results of 6 of them. As a shorthand, we'll often represent the features (first last year, works hard, etc.) using the letters L, M, W and D, and the *feature values* of a particular student as rows of Ts and Fs. So, Richard's feature values correspond to the row $TTFT$, as it is true that he got a first last year and is male, false that he works hard, and so on. The fact that someone, for example, doesn't drink but does work hard can also be represented as a logical expression such as $W \wedge \neg D$.

In the next sections we'll look at how rules like the ones discussed above can be automatically inferred from sets of examples, using the different approaches discussed in the introduction.

7.3 Version Space Learning

The first method essentially treats learning as a search problem. If we make the simplifying assumption that the rule to be learned involves a *conjunction* of facts (i.e., a rule only involving ands and not ors), then there is a fairly limited number of possible rules. A rule like "If they work hard and don't drink a lot they'll get a first" can be represented concisely as the formula $W \wedge \neg D$. (In logic terms, if this formula is true for a particular student, then the rule says that it is true that they will

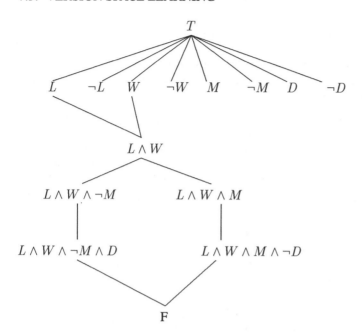

Figure 7.2 *Part of Search Space for Student Problem.*

get a first). The rule "Everyone will get a first" is represented by T (always true), while the rule "No-one will get a first" is represented by F.

All possible such rules can be represented as a *graph* where the top node in the graph is T, the bottom is F, and edges link nodes such that the lower node is the same as the upper node but with an additional condition (e.g., $W \land \neg D$ adds the condition "doesn't drink" to the node W). Part of the graph for the student problem is illustrated in Figure 7.2.

Now, we can think of the learning problem as involving searching this graph to find possible rules that fit the given example data. This can be done by maintaining some candidate *hypotheses* about what the right rules could be, and going through the examples one by one modifying these hypotheses to fit the current example.

A simple version of the approach considers only positive examples (i.e., Alan and Gail), and updates a hypothesis S representing a possible rule covering examples seen so far. S will always be the most specific formula that is true for the examples looked at so far. One formula is more specific than another if it is true for fewer possible examples, and will be below it in the graph. Initially, when no examples have been examined, $S = F$ – i.e., we assume no-one will get a first.

For each positive example we move S up the graph until a formula is found that is true for that example. If there's a choice of more than one such formula the more specific one is chosen.

So, for our student problem, the first example is Alan, with feature values $TTTF$. So looking up the graph, starting at F, a possible new hypothesis is $S =$

$L \wedge W \wedge M \wedge \neg D$ (i.e., only people who got a first last year, work hard, are male AND don't drink will do well this year). Looking at the second example, $TFTT$ and again following up the graph, the most specific formula that fits is $S = L \wedge W$. Other more general formulae are possible given these positive examples (e.g., W) but the most specific one is chosen.

It is also possible to consider just the negative examples, starting at the top of the graph (T). This time a set G of current hypotheses is needed, initially set to just include the node T, so $G = T$. This set will contain the most general formulae that are false for the negative examples. When a negative example is considered we can move down the graph to find formulae that are false for the examples. The most general such formulae are chosen (i.e., true for more examples), but there may be more than one equally general formula.

For the student problem, initially $G = \{T\}$. Once Richard is considered ($TTFT$) possible hypotheses are $G = \{\neg L, W, \neg M, \neg D\}$ (i.e., from the evidence so far possible rules are that you'll get a first if you didn't last year, if you work hard, if you're female, or if you don't go drinking). Considering Alison next ($FFTF$), and moving again down the graph, possible hypotheses include $G = \{\neg L \wedge \neg W, \neg L \wedge M, L \wedge W, \text{etc.}\}$. Considering Jeff ($FTFT$) possibilities include $G = \{\neg L \wedge \neg W \wedge \neg M, L \wedge W, etc.\}$. Finally, considering Simon ($FTTT$), possibilities still include $G = \{\neg L \wedge \neg W \wedge \neg M, L \wedge W, etc.\}$. At the end of this process there are many possible hypotheses (most not explicitly considered above), but including the two rules that you can get a first by NOT getting one last year, NOT working hard and being female, and the more sensible rule that you can get one if you got a first last year and work hard.

Note that the first of these rules contradicts the positive examples, which were completely ignored in the process. In general it is best to consider both positive and negative examples, combining the methods above. Then all the examples can be used to check current hypotheses. A maximally specific hypothesis S is maintained as well as the maximally general hypothesis set G, and at the end of the day the algorithm should give us the range of possible rules, from the most general ones to the most specific. If, at the end of processing, G has ony one element and that equals S then we can be sure there is only one rule that fits the given facts.

The algorithm that combines these techniques is referred to as the candidate elimination algorithm, and is given (in slightly simplified form) below.

- Initialize so that $G = \{T\}, S = F$
- For each example E:

    - If it is a positive example then:
        * If S is false for E, look UP the graph from S and replace S with the first formula which is found true for E.
        * Delete any elements of G which aren't true for E

– If it is a negative example then:

* If any formulae in G are true for E, look DOWN the graph and replace them with the first formulae found which are false for G.
* Delete any elements of G more specific than S.

We can go through how this works out for our full student example. Initially:

$$G = \{T\}$$
$$S = F$$

The first example ($TTFT$) is a negative one. The only element in G is currently T, which is always true, so we look down the graph from T, and find that four nodes have formulae false for that example. These are all added to G, replacing T.

$$G = \{\neg L, W, \neg M, \neg D\}$$
$$S = F$$

Now the positive example ($TTTF$) is considered. S is false for this example, so we look up the graph to find a formula which is true. The one chosen is $L \wedge W \wedge M \wedge \neg D$. (This is the most *specific* such formula, or the first one found looking up the graph from the previous formula.) We also delete any elements of G not true for this example, which will be $\neg L$ and $\neg M$.

$$G = \{W, \neg D\}$$
$$S = L \wedge W \wedge M \wedge \neg D$$

Now we know that, based on just the first two students, the most general rules covering the facts are that anyone who works hard will get a first, or anyone who doesn't drink. The most specific rule covering the facts is that only someone who got a first last year, works hard, is male, and doesn't drink will get a first. Other possible rules fall between these extremes (and between S and an element of G on the graph). For example, another possible rule is that anyone who works hard AND doesn't drink will get a first.

Anyway, after looking at the next two examples ($FFTF$ and $FTFT$), both negative, G becomes:

$$G = \{W \wedge L, W \wedge M, W \wedge D, \neg D \wedge L, \neg D \wedge \neg W, \neg D \wedge M\}$$

There is a slight oddity as G now contains formulae that are false for the previous positive example, as this isn't reconsidered. A more sophisticated version of the algorithm might avoid such problems. Anyway, after considering the positive example ($TFTT$) G gets pruned, as a few elements in G are false for this example, and S gets generalized:

$$G = \{W \wedge L, W \wedge D\}$$
$$S = W \wedge L$$

After the final negative example is considered we get $G = \{W \wedge L\}, S = W \wedge L$, which allows us to conclude for sure that the only rule of the type considered (a simple conjunction of features) is the one given: you'll get a first if you got one last year and work hard.

7.4   Decision Tree Induction

Version space learning works quite nicely if there really is a simple rule there to be learned that can be expressed as a conjunction of facts. But most knowledge isn't quite that simple. More useful rules are likely to contain disjunctions (*or* statements). But there isn't any simple and general way of allowing these in the above method. Maximally specific formula, for example, end up representing rules like "They'll get a first if they're either just like Gail or just like Alan", which hardly capture interesting generalities in the data! Although it is possible to get around the problem by introducing new features – for example, we could have a feature "hard working *or* got a first last year" – this complicates the method and requires that someone predicts which such features might be useful.

The method described in this section provides a way of obtaining a slightly more complex rule involving disjunctions in a fairly straightforward way. It is based on representing the rule as a *decision tree*.

Decision trees are best introduced through an example. Consider Figure 7.3, which is a (much-simplified) decision tree for determining whether someone coming to the surgery with chest pains has had a heart attack. The "diagnosis" is made by going through the tree, answering the yes/no questions posed by the system.

Suppose the answer to the top question (chest pain) is "no". You would follow the branch marked "*no*", and answer the next question (prior history). If the answer to that is "yes", you would answer the question about longest pain episode. Let's say the answer to that question is "no". We therefore conclude that a heart attack is unlikely.

Decision trees provide a natural and intuitive way of representing this kind of knowledge. They are often constructed by hand by experts, and are routinely used in medicine, for example. The same knowledge *could* be represented as a logical formula, but the graphical tree representation is easier to follow. If such structures can be automatically constructed from past data then the resulting knowledge will be easy to verify and apply.

Decision tree induction systems try to construct the *simplest* decision tree that correctly classifies all the example data from past cases. The idea is that if the tree is simple it will capture generalities in the example data and be useful for making predictions or diagnoses given new cases (patients, students, etc.).

One well-established algorithm for inducing decision trees based on available data is ID3. It is based on well-understood statistical techniques (classification

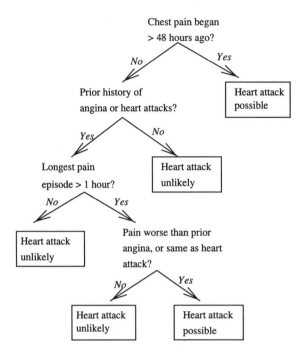

Figure 7.3 *Decision Tree for Diagnosing Heart Attack.*

and regression trees), and has been used in many areas, with various commercial versions of it (and its successor algorithms) available. A typical application might be to induce a decision tree for deciding whether to give someone insurance, based on available data on how much different types of people have claimed!

To illustrate the algorithm we'll go back to the student data, but sneak into the office to change some of last year's results (otherwise the rather trivial result from the last section will be sufficient). The data are repeated here with changes to Richard and Alison's results.

No.	Student	First last year?	Male?	Works hard?	Drinks?	First this year?
1	Richard	yes	yes	no	yes	yes
2	Alan	yes	yes	yes	no	yes
3	Alison	no	no	yes	no	yes
4	Jeff	no	yes	no	yes	no
5	Gail	yes	no	yes	yes	yes
6	Simon	no	yes	yes	yes	no

The general idea in ID3 is to look for features which are particularly good indicators of the result you're interested in. These features are then placed (as

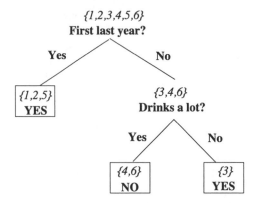

Figure 7.4 *Decision Tree for Student Problem.*

questions) in nodes of the tree. In the above data getting a first last year is the best indicator of whether you'll get a first this year, as all those who got a first last year got one this year and two out of three of those who failed last year failed this year as well. It will therefore be placed as a question at the root node in the tree. (Whether you work hard is another moderately good indicator, while being male or drinking appears to have relatively little to do with it.)

ID3 provides a measure of how good an indicator a particular feature is of the result of interest. This measure is based on information theory, and is described in detail in many of the texts referenced at the end of the chapter[1]. However, to work through the example it is sufficient to use an intuitive notion of which features are better indicators.

The feature which is the best indicator of the result, considering all the examples, is placed as the root node of the decision tree, as illustrated in Figure 7.4. Then the examples are split so that those with different values for the chosen feature are in different sets. In this case the best feature was whether they got a first last year, and based on this the students are split into two groups, $\{1,2,5\}$ and $\{2,4,6\}$.

If it turns out now that all the examples in a group have the same result of interest then that node can be just labelled with the result, as happens for the first such group (students 1, 2 and 5 all get a first). However, if the group contains a mixture of results, the process above must be repeated to find a new feature (but now only considering the smaller group of examples). For students 3, 4 and 6 the best feature to divide them into firsts and non-firsts is, somewhat oddly, whether they drink a lot. The student (Alison) who didn't, gets a first, and the others don't. This in fact

---

[1]For simple binary features and results like in our example, we have the following. For a result of interest R (e.g., gets first) then we can find a score for a feature F: $-P(R \mid F) \times logP(R \mid F) - P(R \mid \neg F) \times logP(R \mid \neg F)$. If we obtain a similar result but for $\neg F$, and take the weighted average of these, according to the number of examples such that F and $\neg F$ are true, then this gives us the total score for that feature, allowing us to assess how good it is as an indicator of R.

completes the decision tree, as all the 'leaves' of the tree contain students who all get the same result.

The resulting decision tree predicts that you'll get a first if either you got one last year OR you didn't get one last year but don't drink much. It could be expressed as a logical formula ($L \vee \neg D$), but the decision tree, as we have said, is an easy graphical representation to verify and apply, and also retains the information that getting a first last year is somehow more important than whether you go drinking. The decision tree also guides the order that questions might be asked when using the derived tree to make new predictions or diagnoses. In this case, first the student would be asked about whether they got a first last year. If they said "yes", no more would be asked. So although the decision tree might give the same results as an equivalent logical expression it is generally more convenient as a representation.

The basic algorithm, illustrated in the above example, can be recursively defined as follows:

To $SelectFeature(Examples)$

- Pick $Feature$ that best splits $Examples$ into different result categories.
- For each $Value$ of $Feature$:

  – Find subset S of $Examples$ such that $Feature = Value$

  – If all examples in S are in same result category then mark the relevant node in the tree with that category else call $SelectFeature$ recursively on S.

The above description covers the case where each feature may have several values and there are several possible results (rather than just yes/no).

Decision tree induction is a fairly powerful yet simple technique which has proved useful in many applications. The resulting decision trees can either be used as is as a simple kind of expert system, or converted into rules and used within a rule-based system.

7.5 Genetic Algorithms

In this section we'll move on to a very different sort of method. A genetic algorithm can be viewed as a kind of search technique. The technique can be applied not only to machine learning problems, but to many other search problems as well. For example, genetic algorithms have been successfully applied to timetabling problems, which involve searching for a possible assignment of events (e.g., lectures) to rooms and times, given various constraints (e.g., people can't be in two places at the same time!). Timetabling is a problem where there are many millions of possible solutions, and it is hard to automatically find the best one. Machine learning, when viewed as a search problem (as outlined in Section 7.3), is similar. There may be many millions of possible rules that MIGHT cover the data provided, and it may be hard to find the best such rules.

Genetic algorithms are biologically inspired, being influenced by theories of *evolution*. Genetic algorithms are also sometimes called *evolutionary algorithms* although this term generally has a slightly broader meaning. The basic idea is to have a population of *genomes* representing possible solutions, to mutate and combine these to produce new ones (*offspring*), and to evaluate the performance of these offspring using some scoring function. The *fittest* of these offspring (with highest score) survive to "mate" again.

This is in fact not so different from the heuristic search algorithms (e.g., best first) discussed in Chapter 4. Here, a successor node (which could be a candidate solution to a problem) was derived from a single parent node. Nodes are scored, and the best ones used to derive further successors. The main difference with genetic algorithms is that new nodes or candidate solutions are derived from two parents rather than one. In some circumstances if two high-scoring parents are chosen the "child" may be REALLY good, and the method allows us to rapidly converge on a solution.

In a bit more detail, if S is the set of candidate concepts/solutions, then the algorithm proceeds as follows:

While S does not include an acceptable solution:

- Score each of the solutions in S.
- Select pairs of solutions from S, favouring pairs with high scores.
- Produce offspring of these pairs by combining and/or mutating the solutions.
- Replace the weakest candidates in S with these offspring.

Typically the initial candidate solutions are selected randomly. Pairs are selected for "breeding" using a semi-random function that favours those with a good score (but which may choose low-scoring ones – it may turn out that you have to mate with a dud to get a great offspring).

Like all heuristic search algorithms genetic algorithms need some way of evaluating candidate solutions. The form of this evaluation function depends greatly on the problem, however for inductive learning problems a simple evaluation function to use is just to measure what proportion of the examples are correctly classified by the rule in question. For example, in the student problem (going back to the original data in Figure 7.1) the rule "If you got a first last year you'll get one this year" works correctly for five out of six students. Only Richard (who doesn't work very hard and drinks a lot) is an exception. The score for this rule would therefore be 5/6.

We also need some way to represent candidate solutions such that they can be mutated and combined in such a way that the results are still meaningful. One approach is to use a fixed length string (or sequence). The string "T#TF" could be used to represent the rule "You'll get a first if you did last year, you work hard, but don't drink". A special character # is used to mean "don't care" (i.e., but it doesn't matter whether you're male or female). This representation can be used to represent any of the types of formulae (involving conjunctions, but not disjunctions) mentioned in Section 7.3.

We now have a way of representing possible solutions, and a way of evaluating how good such a solution is. So we just need methods of generating "offspring" solutions. This is done using the two *genetic operators*: *crossover* and *mutation*. Crossover takes two candidate solutions and swaps over elements to produce two new candidates. The simplest form of this splits each solution in two, and forms two new solutions from the first half of one and the second half of the other, e.g.:

	T # F #
crossed with	F # T F
gives	T # T F
and	F # F #

For our problem we can think of this as mating the category of students who got a first last year but are lazy, with the category that didn't get a first last year but work hard and don't drink, to get one category of students who got a first last year, work hard and don't drink and one category of students who didn't get a first last year and are lazy too.

Anyway, generally if one parent tended to be good because of the first half of the concept representation (say, first last year), and the other parent tended to be good because of the second half (say, hard working), then one of the offspring will typically be better than either parent, and one will be worse than either parent. The latter will tend to be killed off after the next cycle.

The other genetic operator, mutation, involves taking a single candidate and randomly changing some aspect of it (e.g., changing one character randomly to a T, F or #). Using mutation alone would remove the benefits of genetic algorithms, but it generally must be included in case the initial randomly selected population excluded some vital component of the solution.

To briefly run through our student example. We might start off with a sample population of candidate solutions:

S = {#T##, F#TF, TT##, #TT#, ###F}

The first of these corresponds to the rule that you get a first if you are male, the second corresponds to the rule that you get one if you didn't get a first last year but work hard and don't drink beer, and so on.

Each of these can be scored by finding what proportion of the examples are correctly classified. Consider the first candidate solution, #T##. This predicts that all the men will get firsts. But in fact only Alan does. The rule gets only two predictions right (Alan and Alison) so gets a score of 2/6. The next candidate solution has a score of 3/6, and the others scores of 4/6, 4/6 and 3/6.

The best of these are the third and fourth candidate solution, so these are likely to be chosen for crossover. The results will be the solutions TTT# and #T##, replacing the weak candidates #T## and, say, ###F.

S = {TTT#, #T##, F#TF, TT##, ##T#}

The new solutions score 5/6 and 2/6. Now, we could keep on selecting good parents and producing offspring by crossover, but in fact in this example this would never lead to the perfect solution[2]. This is why mutation may be needed: a crucial feature of a solution might just not be present in the examples. So let's suppose mutation is used on the best solution so far. There are many ways it could mutate, and these would normally be selected at random. One of them leads to our perfect scoring solution: T#T#. At which point the algorithm could halt.

For more complicated problems there would be many more candidate solutions at any point, and these would be much more complex. Mutation would obviously be random. Thousands of cycles might be needed before the best solutions appeared. However, this might still be better than conventional search methods.

The critical feature of genetic algorithms is that, by combining two parents by crossover, there is a very high chance that at least one of the offspring will be better than either parent. The method applies most straightforwardly when solutions can be represented as fixed-length strings as above, and where two such representations can be combined by crossover to obtain meaningful new candidate solutions.

As a final, and very different, example of the use of genetic algorithms in learning, imagine that we have a robot with a number of production rules governing its behaviour (e.g., IF next-to-wall THEN turn-round). Suppose we're not sure which of these many possible rules should apply in a given situation. A possible set could be represented as a sequence like TFTFF to mean use just the first and third rules. Now, learning can progress by populating some environment with robots operating under different rules, finding out how well they do, "breeding" the best ones (to get new rule sets to try out) and killing off poor ones. Eventually the best rule set may be found. This doesn't involve inductive learning, as no examples of good robots are provided. It's a kind of learning by experience or experimentation.

7.6 Neural Networks

Neural networks provide a rather different approach to reasoning and learning. A neural network consists of many simple processing units (or *neurons*) connected together. The behaviour of each neuron is very simple, but together a collection of neurons can have sophisticated behaviour and be used for complex tasks. There

---

[2]This assumes that the simple 'split in two' version of crossover is used. In fact this is oversimple, and generally crossover might allow arbitrary portions of each parent solution. For example, it could take the T from the first solution, and the #T# from the last.

are many kinds of neural network, so this discussion will be limited to *perceptrons*, including *multilayer perceptrons*.

In such networks the behaviour of a network depends on *weights* on the connections between neurons. These weights can be *learned* given example data. In this respect, neural networks can be viewed as just another approach to inductive learning problems.

Neural networks are often described as using a *subsymbolic* representation of expert knowledge. There is no meaningful *symbol structure* (e.g., rule or decision tree) produced that can easily be interpreted by an expert, but a collection of simple units that, by the way they are connected and weighted, combine to produce the overall expert behaviour of the system. This means that it is hard to check that the learned knowledge is sensible. To a large degree it has to be treated as a "black box" which, given some inputs, returns some outputs.

Neural networks are biologically inspired, so this section will start with a brief discussion of neurons in the human brain.

7.6.1 Biological Neurons

The human brain consists of approximately ten thousand million simple processing units called neurons. Each neuron is connection to many thousand other neurons. The detailed operation of a neuron is complicated and still not fully understood, but the basic idea is that a neuron receives inputs from its neighbours, and if enough inputs are received at the same time that neuron will be excited or *activated* and *fire*, giving an output that will be received by further neurons.

Figure 7.5 illustrates the basic features of a neuron. The *soma* is the body of the neuron, *dendrites* are filaments that provide inputs to the cell, the *axon* sends output signals, and a *synapse* (or synaptic junction) is a special connection which can be strengthened or weakened to allow more or less of a signal through. Depending on the signals received from all its inputs, a neuron can be in either an excited or inhibited state. If excited, it will pass on that "excitation" through its axon, and may in turn excite neighbouring cells.

The behaviour of a network depends on the strengths of the connections between neurons. In the biological neuron this is determined at the synapse. The synapse works by releasing special chemicals called *neurotransmitters* when it gets an input. More or less of such chemicals may be released, and this quantity may be adjusted over time. This can be thought of as a simple learning process.

7.6.2 The Simple Perceptron: A Basic Computational Neuron

A simple computational neuron based on the above can be easily implemented. It just takes a number of inputs (corresponding to the signals from neighbouring cells), adjusts these using a *weight* to represent the strength of connections at the synapses, sums these, and *fires* if this sum exceeds some threshold. A neuron which

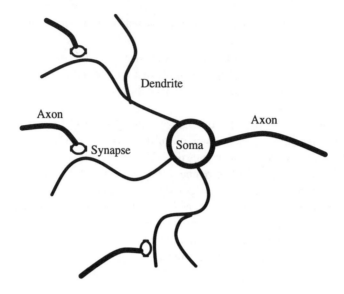

Figure 7.5 *Basic Features of a Biological Neuron.*

fires will have an output value of 1, and otherwise output 0.

More precisely, if there are n inputs (and n associated weights) the neuron finds the weighted sum of the inputs, and outputs 1 if this exceeds a threshold t and 0 otherwise. If the inputs are $x_1 \ldots x_n$, with weights $w_1 \ldots w_n$:

if $w_1 x_1 + \ldots + w_n x_n > t$
then output = 1
else output = 0

This basic neuron is referred to as a simple perceptron, and is illustrated in Figure 7.6. The name "perceptron" was proposed by Frank Rosenblatt in 1962. He pioneered the simulation of neural networks on computers.

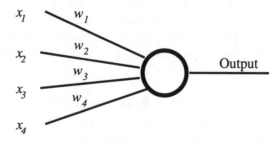

Figure 7.6 *Basic Computational Neuron.*

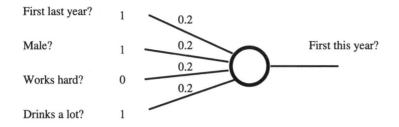

First last year?   1   0.2

Male?   1   0.2

   0.2   First this year?

Works hard?   0

   0.2

Drinks a lot?   1

Figure 7.7 *Neuron with Example Inputs and Weights.*

A serious neural network application would require a network of hundreds or thousands of neurons. However, it is possible to achieve learning even with a single isolated neuron. Learning, in neural networks, involves using example data to adjust the weights in a network. Each example will have specified input–output values. These examples are considered one by one, and weights adjusted by a small amount if the current network gives the incorrect output. The way this is done is to increase the weights on *active* connections[3] if the actual output of the network is 0 but the target output (from the example data) is 1, and decrease the weights if the actual output is 1 and the target is 0. The whole set of examples has to be considered again and again until eventually (we hope) the network *converges* to give the right results for all the given examples.

This will be illustrated using an example before stating the learning algorithm more precisely. Our student example can be used. Each feature (works hard etc.) can be represented by an input, so $x_1 = 1$ if the student in question got a first last year, $x_2 = 1$ if they are male, and so on. The output corresponds to whether they end up getting a first, so $output = 1$ if the student gets a first. Initially the weights are set to some small random values, but to simplify the example we'll assume each weight has the value 0.2. The value of the threshold t also needs to be decided, and we'll make it be 0.5. The amount that the weights are adjusted each time will be called d, and for this example will have the value 0.05.

Figure 7.7 illustrates this, with example data from the first student example (Richard). Before any learning has taken place the output of this network is 1, as the weighted sum of the inputs is 0.2 + 0.2 + 0.2 = 0.6, which is higher than the threshold of 0.5. But Richard didn't get a first! So all the weights on active connections (those with inputs of 1) should be decremented by 0.05. The new weights will be 0.15, 0.15, 0.2 and 0.15.

The next example (Alan) is now considered. His inputs are 1, 1, 1 and 0. The current network gives an output of 0 (the weighted sum is exactly 0.5), but the correct output is 1, so the relevant weights are incremented by d, to give new weights of 0.2, 0.2, 0.25, 0.15. Note how the weight for "works hard" is now higher than the others, while "drinks a lot" is lower: Alan and Richard are pretty similar

---

[3]I.e., those with input values of 1.

in many ways, only Alan works harder than Richard and doesn't drink.

All the other examples are considered in the same way. No adjustments to the weights in the network are needed for Alison, Jeff or Gail. However, after Simon is considered the weights are adjusted to give 0.2, 0.15, 0.2 and 0.1.

Learning doesn't end there. All the examples must be considered again and again until the network gives the right result for as many examples as possible (the *error* is minimized). After a second run-through with our example data the new weights are 0.25, 0.1, 0.2 and 0.1. These weights in fact work perfectly for all the examples, so after the third run-through the process halts. Weights have now been learned such that the perceptron gives the correct output for each of the examples.

If a new student is encountered then to predict their results we use the learned weights. Maybe Tim got a first last year, works hard, is male, but drinks. We would predict that he will get a first.

In this example we can ascribe some meaning to the weights: getting a first last year and working hard are both positive (particularly getting a first), while being male or drinking are less important, with maybe a slightly negative impact. However, for more complex networks it becomes extremely hard to make any sense of the weights; all we know is whether the network gives the right behaviour for the examples.

Anyway, the basic algorithm for all this is as follows:

- Randomly initialize the weights.
- Repeat

    - For each example

        * If the actual output is 1 and the target output is 0, decrement the weights on active connections by d;

        * If the actual output is 0 and the target output is 1, increment the weights on active connections by d;

    until the network gives the correct outputs (or some time limit is exceeded).

Now, although this algorithm worked fine for the student problem, there are some sets of examples where there is just no set of weights that will give the right behaviour. A famous example is the *exclusive or* function, which is meant to output a 1 if one input is 1 and the other is 0, and a 0 otherwise. It's just not possible to find a set of weights for a simple perceptron to implement this function. Minsky and Papert, in their book *Perceptrons*, showed formally in 1969 just what functions simple perceptrons could and couldn't represent. This critique was one of the causes of a decrease of interest in neural networks in the 1970s. Only relatively recently has interest been revived, with more complex versions of the perceptron proposed which don't have the same fundamental limitations. The next section will just briefly sketch a widely used approach.

7.6.3 More Complex Networks and Learning Methods

So far we've just considered what can be done with a single neuron, using the simplest possible method for calculating the output and for learning. This works for some simple examples and illustrates the general idea, but for more complex problems we need to go back to the idea of having an interconnected *network* of neurons (or *units*). These are arranged in layers, with outputs from one layer feeding into inputs in the next layer. We'll consider multilayer *perceptrons*.

Figure 7.8 illustrates a possible (but very small) network with three layers of neurons. This network has an *input layer*, a *hidden layer* and an *output layer*. Each neuron may be connected to several in the next layer (copying its output to the inputs of these units). The input layer does no more than distribute the input values to the next layer and sometimes such a network is referred to as a two-layer network, as the input layer isn't counted. The output layer may consist of several units. This means that the network can calculate (and learn) things where there are several possible answers, rather than just a yes/no decision (maybe distinct units would be used for the results "first", "2-1", "2-2" and "third").

It is possible to have such a network where each unit corresponds to a simple perceptron as described in the previous section. Given some inputs the outputs of the first layer of units would be calculated as before, and these outputs used as the input values for the next layer of units. However, it turns out that if the old rule for calculating the output of a unit is used then there is no good learning method that can be applied. There is no problem with adjusting the weights in the last layer (feeding into the output units); this could be done exactly as before. But it is unclear how the weights between the input and hidden layer should be adjusted. More complex networks may have more than one hidden layer, and here the weights between hidden layers must somehow be obtained.

The *backpropagation* rule, proposed in 1986 by Rumelhart, McClelland and

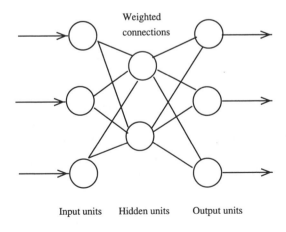

Figure 7.8 *A Small Multilayer Network.*

Williams, specifies how this can be done. The method is substantially more complex than simple perceptron learning, so will not be described fully here; more details are given in the further reading at the end of the chapter. However, the general idea involves first using a slightly more complex function to determine the activation state (and hence output) of a unit. This function, rather than just giving a value of 0 or 1, gives a value between 0 and 1. This means that it is possible to get an idea from the output just how far off the unit is from giving the right answer. In turn, this means that weights can be adjusted more if the output is completely wrong than if the output is almost right. The amount adjusted depends on the *error term* which is just the difference between the target and actual output. This error term can be calculated directly for the final layer of weights, but to adjust weights in earlier layers it has to be *backpropagated* to earlier layers. The error term for units in such layers is calculated by taking a weighted sum of the error terms of the units that it is connected to.

7.6.4   Neural Network Applications

Neural nets are now being (fairly) widely used in practical applications, so it's worth talking briefly about how a neural net application might be developed. This discussion will assume that the *backpropagation* learning rule is to be used in a *multilayer* network. Many other kinds of network and learning methods are possible.

Generally the method can be used whenever we have a lot of training data, and want to produce a system that will give the right outputs for the given inputs in the data. With luck (and judgement) the system will also give sensible outputs for new input combinations which don't exist in the training data.

Although it is possible to use neural networks for many sorts of problems they tend to be particularly useful for *pattern recognition* tasks, such as character recognition. As a simple example of this, suppose we have lots of data corresponding to the digits 0–9 in various different fonts (e.g., 9, *9*, and 9). For each we have a small bitmap corresponding to the digit, and data on which digit it is. We want a system that, given a bitmap image, can recognize which digit it is. One way to set up a neural net for this problem is to have an input unit for each pixel in the bitmap, and an output unit for each digit of interest. (For a given digit we'd require that only the relevant output was activated.) One or more hidden layers could be used between these two. After training with all the example data it should work for new fonts not yet encountered.

To test the trained network it is really necessary to reserve some of the training data to use for testing. So, initially the data available might be split-in-two into training and test data. The network would be trained using the training data, and then tested with the remainder. If it gave good results for the test data (not used in training) this suggests that it will also give good results for new problems (e.g., fonts) for which data is not yet available.

This example application is one where it would be quite hard to write a conventional rule-based system for determining which digit it was, or even to induce a decision tree based on the data, yet humans find it quite easy to recognize characters by visual inspection. Neural networks seem to be good at tasks like this which involve finding patterns in visual or auditory data. Other related applications of neural networks include: learning to pronounce English words; learning to distinguish tanks from rocks in military images; learning to recognize people's handwriting; learning to determine whether someone has had a heart attack given their ECG signal.

Neural networks can also be applied to other kinds of learning problem. One example application is determining whether to give people credit given data on characteristics (e.g., home-owner?) and current creditworthiness. For some of these problems more conventional learning methods (such as ID3, and other statistical methods) can and have been used just as successfully. The methods can be compared by using training and test data as mentioned above and finding out which does best on the test data. However, often what is found is that there isn't that much difference between the results of the different methods, and the results depends more on the example data available and the features chosen than the method used in learning!

Although there are simple commercial neural network tools available that appear as easy to use as a spreadsheet, making best use of the technique requires some understanding of the underlying algorithms. For serious neural network development it is important to consider carefully how to map features of the problem to input/output nodes, what (if any) hidden layers to have in between, what learning method to use, and how to set parameters (such as d and t above). There are no simple rules for all this, so both study and experience is needed. Unfortunately the algorithms involved are fairly mathematical, so making best use of neural net software still requires some mathematical competence.

7.7 Comparing Learning Methods

This chapter has introduced a range of different methods that can be used in learning a general rule or concept from some example data, using a single problem to illustrate each method. There are many other learning methods that could be discussed, and many *statistical* methods that can also be applied.

The different methods can be compared in many ways. We'll just focus on two: the complexity of the knowledge that can be learned, and how well the method can handle *noisy* data.

Each method can learn to classify "concepts" (e.g., students, diseases, digits) given their features. Some of the methods can learn more complex associations between features and category[4]. Neural networks, in particular, can in principle learn an arbitrarily complex function associating inputs and outputs, while version space learning only works well for simple rules involving conjunctions of facts. Decision trees are somewhere in between. Genetic algorithms can be applied to a variety of different concept representations – one can imagine them being used where concepts were represented as decision trees, and the crossover operation involved swapping tree fragments – but do require that parts of a potential solution can be combined in a sensible way.

Some of the methods require that the data contains no oddities or exceptions to the rule that we want to learn. Imagine that we have data on a thousand students. For nine hundred and ninety-nine of them, the rule that "if you work hard and did well last year you'll do well this year" works just fine. But there is one odd one out who has somehow failed this year for whatever reason. Such data is referred to as *noisy*. For most applications we'd still want to learn the rule which works for the vast majority. Yet, in their basic form, many methods would fail to find a solution. Although there is not space to discuss in detail how the methods can be adapted to work, it is easy to see roughly how things might work. It is very hard to adapt version space search for noisy data, but decision tree induction can be adapted if we relax the criterion that a leaf node in the tree must contain examples all of the same result category. We could, for example, mark the node as "Gets a first" even if only 90% of the example students with the given features did. Genetic algorithms can be moderately easily adapted if we give up when we have a sufficiently high (if not perfect) score. Neural networks work well without adaptation.

Although neural networks appear to be winning at this point, at least if we want to learn complex rules given noisy data, they have one clear disadvantage. Neural networks are *opaque*: it is hard to check that the weights correspond to something sensible. Although there are methods being developed to obtain explanations of a neural network's decisions, and to convert neural networks into a more *inspectable* format, these methods are not yet well developed.

So, although the use of neural networks is in many ways the most powerful method described, it may not always be the most appropriate one. It is, in essence, a complex mathematical technique for producing a *classification* system from example data. Other methods can be used, with decision tree induction a particularly appropriate one where a simple and understandable resultant system is required. Other statistical methods should also not be ignored, although not discussed in this book.

For a particular problem or application, the performance of different approaches may be compared using training and test data for that problem. However, for a practical application what is often key is the quality of the data. If you completely forgot to ask the students what grade they got last year then that fact would be unavailable

---

[4]Note that the ability to represent more complex associations may not always be a good thing. If the rule to be learned really is simple, then using a method that can ONLY produce simple rules may work better, especially when there is not much data available to train the system.

to the learning program and NO algorithm could do very well. Similarly, if you only had a small set of atypical example students (maybe a group of friends, who are likely to have features in common) then the resultant system, whatever learning algorithm is used, would not do well given new test data. So it is critical to have a large and representative sample for the examples, and good predictive features. To some extent good features may be discovered by consulting experts in a given field (e.g., asking what symptoms are important for distinguishing diseases). There are also statistical methods that can be used to help determine these. So to make the best use of machine learning methods it may be useful to know some statistics.

Some methods may do well on some problems but very badly on others. So that different methods can be compared across a whole range of problems, large example datasets have been made publicly available. If a new learning method is developed it can be tested on some or all of these to see if it does better on these problems.

7.8 Summary

- Machine learning techniques can be used to automatically produce systems for doing certain *classification* tasks, given examples of cases that have been correctly classified by experts.

- Machine learning can be viewed as involving a *search* for a rule fitting the data. *Version space* learning provides a way of managing this search process. *Genetic algorithms* can be used when the search space would be too big. Genetic algorithms work by combining two moderately good possible solutions to (hopefully) obtain a better "child" solution.

- The learning methods vary in the complexity of the rule that can be learned. Version space learning, for example, cannot easily be used to learn rules involving disjunctions. Neural networks can in principle learn arbitrary functions.

- Decision tree induction is a widely used method that produces the *simplest* decision tree that will correctly classify the training data. The best input feature for splitting examples into different categories is found, and the algorithm called recursively.

- Neural networks learn by repeatedly adjusting weights on links between nodes, until the correct output is given for all the training examples.

- In practice the quality of results may depend more on the training data than the learning method chosen.

7.9 Further Reading

Most longer AI textbooks have a chapter or more on machine learning. There is a fairly detailed account of all the techniques discussed above (and others) in (Luger & Stubblefield, 1993) (ch.12). A slightly more limited discussion is given in (Rich & Knight, 1991) (chs.17–18). Russell & Norvig (Russell & Norvig, 1995) (chs.17–21) give a very sound and comprehensive coverage at quite an advanced level. Ginsberg (Ginsberg, 1993) (ch.15) gives a good but fairly brief and formal account, involving a fair amount of mathematics. Ginsberg says little about neural networks. A good, but fairly formal, logic-based account is included in (Pratt, 1994) (chs.9–10). Neither of the last two say much about genetic algorithms.

There are many books and survey articles devoted to machine learning, genetic algorithms and/or neural networks. Up-to-date recommendations should be available from the AI frequently answered questions lists (see book WWW page for link to this). A fairly light introduction to neural networks is (Beale & Jackson, 1990). *The Encyclopaedia of Artificial Intelligence* (Shapiro, 1992) always contains good short reviews of these and other topics.

7.10 Exercises

1. The following table of data gives information on whether patients were sent home from hospital the day after an operation. Try using *each* of the methods described in this chapter to see if a simple rule or method can be learned for deciding which patients to send home in future. Explain the reasons for any problems with the methods.

Patient	Major Operation?	Family at Home?	Old?	Sent Home?
1	yes	no	no	no
2	yes	no	yes	no
3	no	no	no	yes
4	no	no	yes	no
5	no	yes	yes	yes

2. Problems with version space search can be dealt with by adding a new features "old or major operation" and "family at home or major operation", e.g.,

Patient	Major Op?	Family?	Old?	Old or Major Op?	Family or Major Op?	Sent Home?
1	yes	no	no	yes	yes	no

Show how a correct rule can now be induced using the method.

3. What if we add a sixth patient to the set, with the following data?

Patient	Major Op?	Family?	Old?	Sent Home?
6	no	no	no	no

This patient has identical feature values to patient 3, but was not sent home. Which of the methods do you think would still work for this new dataset? Suggest how decision tree induction might be modified to deal with such cases.

4. Suppose that instead of dividing patients crudely into old and not old we consider instead four age ranges: baby, child, adult, elderly. How might each of the methods be adapted to deal with these *non-binary* features?

5. (Project) Try implementing a simple perceptron (including the learning algorithm). Test it on the student data.

CHAPTER 8

Agents and Robots

Aims:	To introduce intelligent agents, both software agents and physical robots.
Objectives:	You should be able to:
	Describe the capabilities required of an intelligent agent.
	Give three applications of software agents.
	Describe and compare manufacturing robots and autonomous mobile robots, stating what each may be used for.
	Explain why humanoid robots are developed, and how this work contrasts with traditional work in AI.

8.1   Introduction

To conclude this book we'll look at a topic that both provides a linking theme for many of the topics in this book[1], and is interesting in its own right: the design of intelligent agents. An intelligent agent is something that can act independently, with well-defined goals, usually carrying out tasks on behalf of a human user. The agent should be able to adapt what it is doing based on information it receives from its environment or from other agents. A group of agents may operate in the same environment, communicating with each other, sending information or requests. That group of agents might include human "agents".

As a simple example imagine an agent whose task was to do your shopping. The initial goal might be to buy some carrots. The agent must be able to act independently, communicate with other agents (such as the shop assistant), but modify what it is doing in response to what it sees and hears. For example, if it sees some

---

[1]Norvig & Russell (1995) use the concept of intelligent agents as a unifying theme for their whole book.

really nice parsnips, then the goal of getting carrots might be revised. If it drops the carrots/parsnips in a puddle on the way home then it will have to adapt its plan and go back and get some more!

We can divide intelligent agents into software agents, which operate within the confines of the computer (or computer network), and physical agents (i.e., robots) which operate in the physical world and can perceive and manipulate objects in that world.

The design of an intelligent agent may require any of the techniques described in this book. Planning techniques may be used so it can plan what to do, natural language techniques used to communicate with the user, expert system methods used to solve specialized problems, knowledge representation techniques used to represent the required knowledge, vision techniques used to make sense of the physical environment, and learning techniques used so the agent can adapt and improve its behaviour. However, designing an intelligent agent involves new problems. For example, an intelligent agent will normally be acting over an extended period of time, in an environment which may be constantly changing, and where new information received may mean changed priorities. Traditional AI techniques may not be well suited to this, and have to be adapted or rethought. Although there is not scope here to discuss these more recent developments in depth, you should be aware of the problems involved.

The rest of this chapter will briefly look at both software agents and robots, mentioning some of the different techniques that are used.

8.2 Software Agents

A software agent is an independent software component which (typically) provides support for a user of a computer system. For example, software agents can be used as personal assistants to *filter* mail, *find* useful documents, *schedule* meetings, and even do your shopping for you. The user *delegates* responsibility for some of their routine tasks to the agent, who is then responsible for ensuring they are carried out. The agent should have some notion of the user's goals, and be able to carry out the task *autonomously* (making its own decisions, without having to keep going back for precise instructions from the user). The agent might have to communicate with other agents, to find information from its "environment" (e.g., computer files), and adapt what it is doing in response to information received. The agent is constantly active, taking whatever actions are needed at a given time.

The rest of this section will look at a few examples of different kinds of software agent.

8.2.1   Mail Handling Agents

Many people get hundreds of e-mail messages a day. It is hard to sort the important messages from the junk mail that can be safely ignored. Programs that can automatically filter and classify mail are becoming popular.

Sometimes it is not clear whom to send a particular e-mail message to. For example, you might want to send a message to "the person who handles accommodation queries". Here it would be useful to be able to say just that, and have the message automatically forwarded to the appropriate person.

An intelligent agent to handle the e-mail in an organization in this sort of way needs to have some knowledge of the roles and interests of the people in that organization. A simple system might just allow each person to enter rules which specify how mail should be treated (e.g., IF subject-line includes "dinner" THEN priority high; IF subject-line includes "broken" THEN forward-to Fred). A forward chaining inference engine might be used to process the rules and deal with the messages.

An e-mail message consists primarily of natural language text. For an agent to handle such messages properly it should have some understanding of the text. For example, if the message mentioned "fillet steak with gratin dauphinoise" rather than "dinner" it should probably still be given a high priority (although perhaps "pork chops and brussel sprouts" should get a low priority). A full natural language understanding system would probably not be required, just some analysis to try to identify the main topics in the message.

Some systems of this kind use machine learning techniques to adjust the rules based on what the user does with the messages. Perhaps if Mary always ignored messages from John it might induce that for Mary, messages from John should be given a low priority.

A mail handling agent acts autonomously behind the scenes to support the user. It is constantly active, dealing with messages as they arrive. It acts in a changing and unpredictable environment, where mail may arrive at any time and priorities may change with the volume of mail received. Expert system, natural language and machine learning techniques may be used to implement such an agent.

8.2.2   Information Agents

There is now a huge amount of information available on computer networks (such as through the World Wide Web). No-one has time to constantly monitor the information available to see whether new information has appeared that is relevant to them. This task can be delegated to an intelligent agent.

The intelligent agent requires a personal profile giving the user's interests. It can then do repeated searches to try to find information of interest, collate and prioritize the information, and present it to the user on request. This can all be done while the user is getting on with other things. The agent will again be operating in a changing environment, where the information (and the parts of the network) available change from day to day.

The techniques required for this kind of agent are similar to those required for mail handling. Expert system techniques may be required to identify relevant information, machine learning techniques may be used to build and update the personal profile, and possibly natural language techniques used to analyse potentially relevant texts.

8.2.3 Agent-Based Interfaces

One new user interface paradigm is based on the idea that the user communicates with one of a number of *conversational agents*. A conversational agent is an animated "talking head" that the user can communicate with using natural language. For example, the interface to a medical information system might consist of a facial image recognizable as a doctor. The interface to a mail system might consist of a facial image recognizable as a postman. The user will be able to talk to these interface agents (in an anthropomorphic fashion) and get a response back, perhaps through speech, with the facial expressions of the interface agents reflecting the content of the response!

An interface agent may use information about the user's particular needs and preferences and factual information about the user and the organization. For example, the user might want to be able to say something like "Send this memo to all my customers in Edinburgh", and have the appropriate action done. For this to be possible the system would clearly need to be able to interpret the sentence and then access the relevant customer list.

An interface agent may also need to communicate with other agents in a system, such as mail and information handling agents. For example, an interface agent might *request* an information agent to go and find information on a given topic. Special languages have been designed to allow such communication between interacting agents, and knowledge representation formalisms developed to allow different agents to share their knowledge. *Agent-oriented programming* is a programming paradigm that encourages thinking in terms of communicating agents rather than simply programming modules or applications.

Interface agents may use AI techniques, such as natural language processing, machine learning, and knowledge representation. However, the anthropomorphic talking head is becoming popular as an interface idea in its own right, whether or not any intelligence is associated with it. For example, in computer games online help is sometimes presented via a talking head. The concept of an intelligent agent may therefore be more a metaphor than a reality. You communicate with the system *as if* you were communicating to an intelligent entity with a particular appearance and personality, but there may in fact be very little intelligence and certainly no personality behind the system!

8.3 Robots

The term "robot" is used for anything from the relatively simple programmable manipulators used for tasks such as car assembly, to the intelligent *humanoid* robots found in science fiction. The more sophisticated robots may be viewed as intelligent agents, operating in the physical world. The robot will be carrying out tasks for a human, but will have its own goals and will be able to adapt its behaviour based on information received. The main difference between a robot and a software agent is that the robot will be able to perceive (by vision) objects in a physical environment, and will be able to manipulate objects in that environment.

The main difficulty in designing robots is that the real world is messy. It is easy to write a planning program that can, in theory, work out how to move objects between rooms (Chapter 4). But in reality there may be objects in the way of the robot (maybe a coffee table), the environment changes (a human may sneak in and move the table), the robot's actions aren't precise (how much did it move forward when the wheels slipped on the carpet?), and its visual perceptions uncertain (is that a waste paper bin or a spin drier?). So, designing a robot that can carry out even a simple task may be very complex.

The design of a robot depends very much on the task it is designed for. For some tasks, such as manufacturing, the physical environment may be fairly fixed and predictable. Here, a relatively dumb robot may be sufficient, with little flexibility. For other tasks much more flexibility is required. For example, robots are now used to explore or clean up in inhospitable environments where humans cannot safely go. Robots for these tasks must be *mobile*, *autonomous* (deciding for itself, to some extent, what to do next), be able to cope with unpredicted occurrences and recover from errors.

This section will look at different types of robot developed for different purposes: manufacturing robots; autonomous mobile robots; and humanoid robots (designed in the image of man).

8.3.1 Manufacturing Robots

Robots are currently used in a variety of manufacturing tasks, such as welding, assembly and spray painting. Currently most of these robots are pretty dumb – they just repeatedly execute some standard sequence of actions. This can work fairly well as the robot's environment can be designed so that nothing unexpected occurs and everything is in its expected place.

A manufacturing robot typically consists of a jointed *arm* with a device or *end effector* at the end of it, such as a *gripper* (to pick things up), a paint sprayer or a welding gun. The number and arrangement of the joints determines the range of positions and orientations that the end effector can be positioned in. For full flexibility you need six joints, which allows the effector to be placed in any position within reach, at any angle. (It has six degrees of freedom, three for x-y-z position

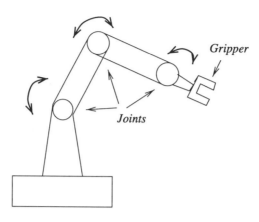

Figure 8.1 *A Basic Robot Arm.*

and three for orientation.) Figure 8.1 illustrates a simpler arm, with just three joints and able to operate just in one plane.

To get a basic manufacturing robot to do what you want you have to program it. At a minimum, this might just consist of telling it a position to move to and an action to take (e.g., move gripper to position P, orientation θ and close it). Calculations are then done to work out exactly how to move the various joints so that the gripper is positioned correctly, motors start whirring, and the arm moves.

If the robot is to do a complex sequence of actions then programming the robot in this way is quite tedious – each position and orientation has to be precisely specified. A common approach is therefore to program a robot by first moving it by hand through the desired sequence of actions and having the movements stored so they can be repeated.

Even a basic manufacturing robot may obtain some information from the environment and adapt its behaviour accordingly. A very simple aspect of this is the use of force sensing to determine how firmly an object is grasped. If the robot is picking up something delicate like an egg, then clearly just closing the gripper using all its strength is not going to be a good idea! Most robot grippers can therefore detect, using simple strain gauges, what the pressure is on the object gripped. This is a simple example of using *touch* as a source of information about the environment.

A manufacturing robot may also use some basic visual data from a camera. However, because the robot's environment can be set up to make things easy, the methods used may be quite simple. For example, a "stripe" of light can be projected onto a (carefully positioned) three-dimensional object. The contour of that stripe in the image will give a clearly recognizable "signature" for each object, making recognition easy.

Although manufacturing robots may, in a basic way, receive information from the environment and adapt their behaviour accordingly, most of the issues in their development are engineering and organizational ones rather than AI issues. So we'll now move on to a more interesting class of robot: the autonomous mobile robot.

8.3.2   Autonomous Mobile Robots

The manufacturing robots discussed above were just arms attached to a fixed base. However, many applications require robots that can move around. For example, mobile robots are being used as "delivery boys" in large organizations. They can be instructed to take some object to some location somewhere in the building, navigate their way about the building (avoiding obstacles on the way) and make the delivery. Mobile robots may also be used to do routine tasks in hazardous environments, such as the surface of Mars, the dangerous bits of a nuclear power station, or near a fire.

Mobile robots are often small unmanned land vehicles. However, underwater and even aerial vehicles have also been developed. Autonomous aerial vehicles may be used, for example, to deliver food and medical supplies to refugees in a war zone, where human pilots are reluctant to fly. Underwater vehicles may be used, for example, for oil exploration and the maintenance of rigs. Figure 8.2 is an example of an autonomous underwater robot used for oil exploration.

Mobile robots may sometimes be remotely operated by a human who can see what the robot sees through its camera, and can directly control the movement and actions of the robot. However, this clearly requires the constant attention of a human operator. It wouldn't be much help, for example, for a mail delivery robot, as the human operator could just as easily deliver the mail himself. It is there-

Figure 8.2   *The Rover Underwater Autonomous Robot. (Image provided by the Ocean Systems Laboratory, Department of Computing and Electrical Engineering, Heriot-Watt University.)*

fore better if mobile robots have at least some degree of autonomy, can navigate and avoid obstacles without assistance, make routine decisions, and to some extent deal with unexpected events. Such robots fit well with our definition of intelligent agents. They may occasionally have to call upon a human operator for advice or instructions, but are essentially independent entities with their own goals.

Mobile robots normally operate in dynamic and unpredictable environments. The ability to perceive that environment, and to take appropriate actions, is therefore vital. For some applications this might be very simple. For example, mail delivery robots might follow clear marked tracks in a known environment, with their obstacle avoidance skills limited to stopping in their tracks when they detect something moving in front of them. However, other applications might require more sophisticated methods. They might have to be able to navigate around obstacles in rough unknown terrain, maybe construct an internal map of that terrain, and be able to plan appropriate actions. A firefighting robot, for example, would have to find its way around the building (or forest), determine where the fire is, and possibly make decisions about whether to rescue people/objects or take firefighting actions.

To some extent, classical AI techniques, as introduced in this book, may be used in mobile robotics. For example, an early mobile robot, Shakey, could use planning and search techniques to work out how to get from one room to another, given a model of the world, but specialized low-level routines to actually carry out the actions. Vision techniques may be used to check and update the world model. However, some recent work has questioned the classical AI approach. In the classical approach you work with a symbolic model of the world, plan what to do, then do it. Some recent research advocates throwing out the world model (which is almost certainly inaccurate) and working at a level of more primitive actions, responding directly to perceptions from the environment. For example, it is possible to program a robot to avoid obstacles or find its way around the walls of a room without ever using any internal representation of that room. These tasks or *behaviours* (such as obstacle avoidance) may be used as the basic primitives of the new approach.

8.3.3 Humanoid Robots

An autonomous mobile robot, as we can see from Figure 8.2, looks little like the human-like robots of science fiction. Although they may do useful tasks, it is unclear how much they tell us about how humans reason about and manipulate their environment. So there is some work on developing human-like robots, complete with head, eyes, arms, hands, fingers and possibly even legs. Some claim that by building complete robots, which can interact with their surroundings in much the same way as humans can, will result in more progress towards understanding human intelligence and producing more general-purpose intelligent systems. This approach contrasts with the more traditional approach in Artificial Intelligence of

Figure 8.3 *Cog the Robot.*

focusing on a particular task, such as planning or vision, and developing sophisticated isolated programs able to deal with complex, but idealized problems.

One example humanoid robot is "Cog" developed at MIT (Massachusetts Institute of Technology) by Rodney Brooks and team. Cog has a human-like arm
(with springy joints with similar properties to human joints), a torso that allows it
to bend over, twist around etc., a head mounted on a flexible neck, and two active
"eyes" that can point in different directions (see Figure 8.3). Cog isn't terribly intelligent as yet, but by starting with a human-like physical architecture interesting
problems are being addressed, such as how we swivel our eyes to focus on interesting objects. These basic skills are similar to those a human baby learns in its first
few weeks. The philosophy behind Cog is that, to automate human intelligence,
it is better to start by building a complete human-like system with the abilities of
a human baby (or even an insect!), and progress from there, rather than concen-
trate on "adult" versions of isolated skills, and then hope that we will be able to
eventually glue the various components together. The hope is that a robot able to
interact with its environment in all the complex ways that a human can will be able
to *learn* the more advanced skills, rather than have them pre-programmed into it as
symbolic reasoning programs.

8.4   Conclusion

This final chapter has rather briefly introduced the topic of intelligent agents, both
software agents and physical agents (or robots). Intelligent agents both have practical applications, and also may use the range of AI techniques introduced in this
book, from knowledge representation to vision.

The development of complete autonomous agents operating in a real environment (whether the physical environment, or a computer network) introduces new problems in Artificial Intelligence. Early work focused on manipulating symbolic representations of the physical world, but these representations were idealized (perfect, predictable), and it was never clear how a physical robot doing real tasks would obtain these symbolic models based on their interactions with real objects in the world.

Recent AI research is now therefore more concerned with coping with unpredictability, uncertainty and change. While the traditional work described in this book has led to useful practical systems, it seems likely that this more recent emphasis on coping with interactions in the real world is likely to lead both to better practical systems and a better understanding of human intelligence.

8.5 Summary

- Intelligent agents are independently operating computational systems that operate in some environment, and can adapt their behaviour given new information received.
- *Autonomous* agents can, to some extent, make their own decisions without reference to a human user.
- They can be divided into software agents, which operate in the world of computers and networks, and physical agents, or robots, which operate in the physical world.
- Software agents can act as personal assistants, handling mail, retrieving information, or just providing a human-like interface to application programs.
- *Autonomous mobile robots* are mobile physical agents that operate independently in the physical world. Typical tasks include delivering goods in buildings and retrieving objects from inhospitable environments.
- The development of agents operating in real environments has led to a change in emphasis in recent work in AI, with more emphasis on uncertainty, change, and managing simple tasks in realistic scenarios.

8.6 Further Reading

Russell & Norvig use intelligent agents as a theme throughout their book (Russell & Norvig, 1995), and have one chapter devoted to robotics. Most other AI texts include relatively little material. Most current textbooks on robotics emphasize the engineering issues, and focus on robot arms. However, among these, a particularly comprehensive text is McKerrow's *Introduction to Robotics* (McKerrow, 1991), which includes some material on mobile robots and AI related issues.

For not-too-technical introductions to current work in Artificial Intelligence it is probably best to look at recent issues of the journals *AI Magazine* or *Artificial Intelligence Review*. The *AI Journal* has more technical and specialist articles.

8.7 Exercises

1. Suggest a design for a basic intelligent agent for monitoring and selecting articles from newsgroups that might be of interest. How would you allow people to describe their interests? How could articles be matched given these interests? How could the user profile be updated based on information about which articles the user actually chose to read?

2. Suppose you are to design a robot that is to be able to navigate across a room. There are various large items of furniture in the room. Suggest two possible approaches, one which makes use of an internal model of the room, and one which does not use any such model.

3. How could the robot make use of *touch* or *vision* systems in each approach?

4. Suppose someone sneaked in and moved the furniture. Which approach would be more *robust* in dealing with this changed environment?

5. A simple planner (as described in Chapter 4) may be used to find a sequence of actions to collect various objects from different rooms and deliver them to specified locations, given a simple representation of the building. Assume the robot can reliably get from one room to a neighbouring one, and that it has available (via a vision system) the ability to detect whether a specified object is in the room. Suggest an algorithm for *executing* the plan, which includes *monitoring* actions to check that the state of the world is as expected. If an object is not in its expected place the system should *replan* to find a new way to complete its task, but ignoring the misplaced object.

6. Find recent issues of *AI Magazine, Artificial Intelligence Review*, or similar. Note how many articles deal with uncertainty or change.

Glossary

Agent: Entity that perceives, reasons and acts within some external environment (e.g., intelligent agent).

Alpha-Beta pruning: Method for improving the efficiency of minimax search used for game playing systems.

Autonomous: Able to function without external control or intervention (e.g., autonomous agent; autonomous mobile robot).

Backpropagation: A learning algorithm used for neural networks.

Backtracking: Returning to a previous choice point in a search, in order to explore other alternatives.

Backward chaining: Method used in problem solving which involves starting with a goal or hypothesis and working backwards using rules to find what facts are necessary to prove the goal.

Bayes' theorem: Rule for calculating the probability of a hypothesis given some evidence, based on other available probabilities.

Best first: Search strategy which uses heuristics to guide search, looking at the most promising nodes first.

Breadth first: Search strategy that involves exploring all nodes in a tree at a given depth (from root) before exploring nodes further down in tree.

Brute force: Search strategy not using any intelligence or heuristics.

Case-specific data: Data specific to a particular problem or case (e.g., data on a particular patient) in an expert system.

Certainty factors: Measure of the likelihood that a fact or conclusion is true, often used in rule-based expert systems.

Chinese room: Thought experiment proposed by Searle to demonstrate that a system could behave intelligently without being intelligent.

Class: Group of items with similar characteristics.

Classification: Assigning an object to a particular category or class based on its features.

Combinatorial explosion: Term used to indicate a problem with exponential complexity, where increasing the size of a problem by a small amount causes an "explosion" in the number of possibilities to be considered when looking for a solution.

Compositional semantics: Method for finding the meaning of a sentence by combining the meanings of its syntactic constituents.

Condition-action rule: Term sometimes used for rules in expert systems, where some action should be taken whenever a condition is satisfied.

Conditional probability: Probability of something being true given some evidence.

Conflict resolution strategy: Method for deciding which rule to fire when more than one have their conditions satisfied. Used in forward chaining rule-based systems.

Continuous speech: Natural speech without deliberate pauses.

Data driven: Search or inference that starts with the data and tries to work forward to draw new conclusions or find a goal. Contrast with goal driven; see also **Forward chaining**.

Decision tree: Tree structure where each node is labelled with a test or question, each branch with the possible answers, and leaf nodes with some decision or solution. By traversing the tree answering questions and following appropriate branches, leaf nodes are reached and a decision can be made.

Declarative: Representing *what* is true rather than *how* something should be done (cf. **Procedural**).

Default value: Value given to something in the absence of more specific information.

Depth first: Search strategy that involves exploring a given branch of a search tree to its full length before exploring other branches.

Difference operator: Function used to find edges in an image based on differences in intensity values in nearby pixels.

Domain: Subject area (e.g., medicine). In logic it has a quite different meaning, relating to the set of objects considered when specifying the meaning of a statement.

Dynamic time warping: Method used in speech recognition to adjust for the fact that words can be spoken at different speeds.

Edge detection: Computer vision technique. Detecting rapid changes in brightness in an image, possibly corresponding to edges of objects.

Expert system: System embodying specialist expertise (e.g., medical knowledge).

Expert system shell: Skeletal expert system program allowing new expert systems to be (relatively) easily built by adding new expert knowledge.

Explanation system: Component of expert system, used in providing explanations or rationale for the conclusions drawn by the system.

Forward chaining: Method used in problem solving which involves applying rules starting with the data and drawing conclusions from that data (cf. **Backward chaining**).

Frame: Record-like structure used to represent knowledge. A frame is used to represent simple facts about an object or class as slots and slot values, and inheritance used to make inferences.

Frequency spectrogram: Shows the amount of energy in different frequency ranges (e.g., given some recorded speech).

Game tree: Tree representing all the possible moves in a game, usually down to some depth limit.

Genetic algorithm: Search algorithm used in machine learning which involves generating new candidate solutions by combining two high-scoring "parents".

Goal driven: Inference method that starts with the hypothesis or goal and works backwards to the data.

Heuristic: Generally, used to refer to "rules of thumb" used to provide intelligent guesses concerning what to do. In search, used more specifically to refer to an estimate of the cost or distance from a given node to a solution.

Heuristic search: Search methods using heuristics.

Hierarchy: Tree structure where more general (or dominating) classes or objects come above the classes or objects which they dominate.

Hill climbing: Search strategy involving always pursuing the best successor of the current node.

Hough transform: Method for finding features (e.g., lines) in an image by finding how many edge points fall on each possible feature.

Inductive learning: Learning a general rule from a set of example cases (with solutions).

Inference engine: Part of expert system responsible for drawing new inferences given the current data and goals.

Inference rule: Rule stating what can be validly concluded from existing facts in a logic (e.g., modus ponens).

Inferential adequacy: The ability of a system to draw a range of different kinds of inferences.

Inheritance: Inference of new facts by assuming that what is true about general classes is also (usually) true for subclasses and instances of a class.

Knowledge acquisition: The acquisition of specialist knowledge from experts, in a form that can be used in an expert system.

Knowledge base: Collection of facts and rules capturing specialist knowledge in an expert system.

Knowledge engineer: AI specialist concerned with expert system development.

Likelihood ratios: Ratio expressing conditional probabilities in a form that simplifies certain calculations.

Machine learning: Automatic learning of new knowledge from, for example, past cases, experience or exploration.

Means–ends analysis: Problem-solving method which tries to find actions that reduce difference between current state and goal.

Minimax: Game playing algorithm based on assumption that opponent will try to minimize your advantage at each move.

Morphology: Study of the form and structure of words.

Multiple inheritance: Inheritance from several different sources (when a class may have multiple parents).

Natural language: A human language (like English) rather than a computer language.

Parse tree: Tree representation of syntactic structure of sentence.

Pattern recognition: Class of methods for identifying the category to which an object belongs based on its (often visual) pattern (e.g., identifying letters in handwriting from an image).

Perceptron: Simple neural network.

Phoneme: Basic unit of speech; part of word (e.g., "t").

Pixel: Point-like, basic element of a digital image.

Pragmatics: Stage of language analysis that takes account of the context in which things are said.

Predicate logic: A logic widely used in AI for representing knowledge.

Procedural: Representing *how* something should be done (procedures) rather than *what* is true (cf. **Declarative**).

Production rule: Term used for IF–THEN rules in rule-based expert systems. (Meaning of term slightly different in other areas of Computer Science.)

Proof theory: Theory stating what inferences are valid in a logic.

Reason maintenance: Recording the justifications for conclusions, so when a fact is withdrawn all the facts that are derived from it are also withdrawn.

Representational adequacy: Ability to represent complex facts.

Resolution: A rule of inference and simple proof procedure based on that rule of inference. Used in the Prolog programming language.

Robot: System able to manipulate physical objects in the world, usually with the aid of sensors.

Rule-based system: Expert system based on using IF–THEN rules for representing knowledge.

Search space: Set of all possible nodes to be considered in a given search problem (usually those reachable from some start node).

Search strategy: Strategy for controlling the search (of a graph or tree) for some target node or state.

Search tree: Tree representation of search space, showing how possible solutions may be reached from some initial state.

Semantic network: Knowledge representation scheme based on networks of nodes and links, normally representing objects and relationships between objects.

Semantics: The meaning of a statement (whether a natural language sentence, statement in a programming language, or statement in a logic). Also used to refer to the stage of natural language understanding concerned with deriving sentence meaning.

Speech act: Action performed by spoken utterance (e.g., command).

Speech recognition: The recognition of word sequences from a speech signal.

Speech understanding: Determining sentence meaning from a speech signal.

State space: Set of problem states reachable, given a problem to be solved using state space search.

State space search: Solving a problem by searching through the possible problem states that may be reached from some initial state.

Subsymbolic: Representation of knowledge such that there are no meaningful "symbol structures" (e.g., neural networks).

Symbol structures: Data structures composed of symbols denoting objects or concepts. Most AI knowledge is represented in this way.

Syntax: Legal organizations of constituents in a language. For example, the syntax of English defines legal combinations of words in a sentence. Also used to refer to stage of natural language understanding concerned with ascertaining the structure of a sentence.

Turing test: Test proposed to check for human-like intelligence by comparing a computer program's ability to answer arbitrary questions with that of a human.

Version space learning: Inductive learning method based on a particular algorithm for searching a space of hypotheses.

Working memory: Part of expert system used to represent facts that are currently believed true about the problem being worked on.

References

J. F. Allen. *Natural Language Understanding*. Benjamin/Cummings, Redwood City, California, 1995.

D. H. Ballard and C. M. Brown. *Computer Vision*. Prentice Hall, Englewood Cliffs, New Jersey, 1982.

A. Barr and E. A. Feigenbaum (editors).*The Handbook of Artificial Intelligence*. HeurisTech Press and William Kaufmann, Stanford, California and Los Altos, California, 1982.

R. Beale and T. Jackson. *Neural Computing: An Introduction*. Institute of Physics Publishing, Bristol, UK, 1990.

I. Bratko. *Prolog Programming for Artificial Intelligence (second edition)*. Addison-Wesley, Reading, Massachusetts, 1990.

B. G. Buchanan and E. H. Shortliffe (editors). *Rule-Based Expert Systems: The MYCIN Experiments of the Stanford Heuristic Programming Project*. Addison-Wesley, Reading, Massachusetts, 1984.

F. T. de Dombal. Computer-aided decision support – the obstacles to progress. *Methods of Information in Medicine*, 26:183–184, 1987.

T. Dean. *Artificial Intelligence: Theory and Practice*. Benjamin/Cummings, Redwood City, California, 1995.

G. Gazdar and C. Mellish. *Natural Language Processing in Prolog*. Addison-Wesley, Reading, Massachusetts, 1989.

M. Ginsberg. *Essentials of Artificial Intelligence*. Morgan Kaufmann, Los Altos, California, 1993.

D. E. Heckerman, E. J. Horvitz, and B. N. Nathwani. Torwards normative expert systems: Part I. The Pathfinder project. *Methods of Information in Medicine*, 31(2): 90–105, 1992.

J. Holmes. *Speech Synthesis and Recognition*. Van Nostrand Reinhold, Wokingham, UK, 1988.

P. Jackson. *Introduction to Expert Systems (second edition)*. Addison-Wesley, Reading, Massachusetts, 1990.

R. C. Jain. *Machine Vision*. McGraw-Hill, New York, 1995.

P. Lucas and L. van der Gaag. *Principles of Expert Systems*. Addison-Wesley, Wokingham, UK, 1991.

G. F. Luger and W. A. Stubblefield. *Artificial Intelligence: Structures and Strategies for Complex Problem Solving*. Benjamin/Cummings, Redwood City, California, 1993.

D. Marr. *Vision*. W. H. Freeman and Company, San Francisco, California, 1982.

P. J. Mckerrow. *Introduction to Robotics*. Addison-Wesley, Wokingham, UK, 1991.

R. A. Miller, H. E. Pople, and J. D. Myers. Internist-I, an experimental computer-based diagnostic consultant for general internal medicine. *The New England Journal of Medicine*, 307:468–476, 1982.

V. S. Nalwa. *A Guided Tour of Computer Vision*. Addison-Wesley, Reading, Massachusetts, 1993.

F. C. N. Pereira and S. M. Shieber. *Prolog and Natural Language Analysis*. Center for the Study of Language and Information (CSLI), Stanford, California, 1987.

I. Pratt. *Artificial Intelligence*. Macmillan, Basingstoke, UK, 1994.

E. Rich and K. Knight. *Artificial Intelligence*. McGraw-Hill, New York, 1991.

S. Russell and P. Norvig. *Artificial Intelligence: A Modern Approach*. Prentice Hall, Englewood Cliffs, New Jersey, 1995.

J. R. Searle. Minds, brains and programs. *Behavioural and Brain Sciences*, 3: 417–457, 1980.

S. C. Shapiro. *Encyclopaedia of Artificial Intelligence*. Wiley, New York, 1992.

E. Turban. *Expert Systems and Applied Artificial Intelligence*. Macmillan, New York, 1992.

A. M. Turing. Computing machinery and intelligence. *Mind*, 59: 433–460, 1950.

Index